WILLIAM SHAKESPEARE was born in Stratford-upon-Avon in April, 1564, and his birth is traditionally celebrated on April 23. The facts of his life, known from surviving documents, are sparse. He was one of eight children born to John Shakespeare, a merchant of some standing in his community. William probably went to the King's New School in Stratford, but he had no university education. In November 1582, at the age of eighteen, he married Anne Hathaway, eight years his senior, who was pregnant with their first child, Susanna. She was born on May 26, 1583. Twins, a boy, Hamnet (who would die at age eleven), and a girl, Judith, were born in 1585. By 1592 Shakespeare had gone to London, working as an actor and already known as a playwright. A rival dramatist, Robert Greene, referred to him as "an upstart crow, beautified with our feathers." Shakespeare became a principal shareholder and playwright of the successful acting troupe the Lord Chamberlain's men (later, under James I, called the King's men). In 1599 the Lord Chamberlain's men built and occupied the Globe Theatre in Southwark near the Thames River. Here many of Shakespeare's plays were performed by the most famous actors of his time, including Richard Burbage, Will Kempe, and Robert Armin. In addition to his 37 plays, Shakespeare had a hand in others, including *Sir Thomas More* and *The Two Noble Kinsmen,* and he wrote poems, including *Venus and Adonis* and *The Rape of Lucrece.* His 154 sonnets were published, probably without his authorization, in 1609. In 1611 or 1612 he gave up his lodgings in London and devoted more and more of his time to retirement in Stratford, though he continued writing such plays as *The Tempest* and *Henry VIII* until about 1613. He died on April 23, 1616, and was buried in Holy Trinity Church, Stratford. No collected edition of his plays was published during his lifetime, but in 1623 two members of his acting company, John Heminges and Henry Condell, published the great collection now called the First Folio.

Bantam Shakespeare
The Complete Works—29 Volumes
Edited by David Bevington
With forewords by Joseph Papp on the plays

The Poems: Venus and Adonis, The Rape of Lucrece, The
Phoenix and Turtle, A Lover's Complaint,
the Sonnets

Antony and Cleopatra	*The Merchant of Venice*
As You Like It	*A Midsummer Night's Dream*
The Comedy of Errors	*Much Ado about Nothing*
Hamlet	*Othello*
Henry IV, Part One	*Richard II*
Henry IV, Part Two	*Richard III*
Henry V	*Romeo and Juliet*
Julius Caesar	*The Taming of the Shrew*
King Lear	*The Tempest*
Macbeth	*Twelfth Night*

Together in one volume:

Henry VI, Parts One, Two, and Three
King John and Henry VIII
*Measure for Measure, All's Well that Ends Well, and
Troilus and Cressida*
Three Early Comedies: Love's Labor's Lost, The Two
Gentlemen of Verona, The Merry
Wives of Windsor
Three Classical Tragedies: Titus Andronicus, Timon
of Athens, Coriolanus
The Late Romances: Pericles, Cymbeline, The Winter's
Tale, The Tempest

Two collections:

Four Comedies: The Taming of the Shrew, A Midsummer
Night's Dream, The Merchant of Venice,
Twelfth Night
Four Tragedies: Hamlet, Othello, King Lear, Macbeth

William Shakespeare

ROMEO AND JULIET

Edited by
David Bevington

David Scott Kastan,
James Hammersmith,
and Robert Kean Turner,
Associate Editors

With a Foreword by
Joseph Papp

BANTAM BOOKS
NEW YORK·TORONTO·LONDON·SYDNEY·AUCKLAND

ROMEO AND JULIET

*A Bantam Book / published by arrangement
with Scott, Foresman and Company*

PUBLISHING HISTORY

*Scott, Foresman edition published / January 1980
Bantam edition, with newly edited text and substantially revised,
edited, and amplified notes, introductions, and other
materials, published / February 1988
Valuable advice on staging matters has been
provided by Richard Hosley.
Collations checked by Eric Rasmussen.
Additional editorial assistance by Claire McEachern.*

ISBN 0-553-21305-9 (pbk.)

Published simultaneously in the United States and Canada

PRINTED IN THE UNITED STATES OF AMERICA

OPM   29   28   27   26   25   24

Contents

Foreword

It's hard to imagine, but Shakespeare wrote all of his plays with a quill pen, a goose feather whose hard end had to be sharpened frequently. How many times did he scrape the dull end to a point with his knife, dip it into the inkwell, and bring up, dripping wet, those wonderful words and ideas that are known all over the world?

In the age of word processors, typewriters, and ballpoint pens, we have almost forgotten the meaning of the word "blot." Yet when I went to school, in the 1930s, my classmates and I knew all too well what an inkblot from the metal-tipped pens we used would do to a nice clean page of a test paper, and we groaned whenever a splotch fell across the sheet. Most of us finished the school day with ink-stained fingers; those who were less careful also went home with ink-stained shirts, which were almost impossible to get clean.

When I think about how long it took me to write the simplest composition with a metal-tipped pen and ink, I can only marvel at how many plays Shakespeare scratched out with his goose-feather quill pen, year after year. Imagine him walking down one of the narrow cobblestoned streets of London, or perhaps drinking a pint of beer in his local alehouse. Suddenly his mind catches fire with an idea, or a sentence, or a previously elusive phrase. He is burning with impatience to write it down—but because he doesn't have a ballpoint pen or even a pencil in his pocket, he has to keep the idea in his head until he can get to his quill and parchment.

He rushes back to his lodgings on Silver Street, ignoring the vendors hawking brooms, the coaches clattering by, the piteous wails of beggars and prisoners. Bounding up the stairs, he snatches his quill and starts to write furiously, not even bothering to light a candle against the dusk. "To be, or not to be," he scrawls, "that is the—." But the quill point has gone dull, the letters have fattened out illegibly, and in the middle of writing one of the most famous passages in the history of dramatic literature, Shakespeare has to stop to sharpen his pen.

Taking a deep breath, he lights a candle now that it's dark, sits down, and begins again. By the time the candle has burned out and the noisy apprentices of his French Huguenot landlord have quieted down, Shakespeare has finished Act 3 of *Hamlet* with scarcely a blot.

Early the next morning, he hurries through the fog of a London summer morning to the rooms of his colleague Richard Burbage, the actor for whom the role of Hamlet is being written. He finds Burbage asleep and snoring loudly, sprawled across his straw mattress. Not only had the actor performed in *Henry V* the previous afternoon, but he had then gone out carousing all night with some friends who had come to the performance.

Shakespeare shakes his friend awake, until, bleary-eyed, Burbage sits up in his bed. "Dammit, Will," he grumbles, "can't you let an honest man sleep?" But the playwright, his eyes shining and the words tumbling out of his mouth, says, "Shut up and listen—tell me what you think of *this*!"

He begins to read to the still half-asleep Burbage, pacing around the room as he speaks. ". . . Whether 'tis nobler in the mind to suffer the slings and arrows of outrageous fortune—"

Burbage interrupts, suddenly wide awake, "That's excellent, very good, 'the slings and arrows of outrageous fortune,' yes, I think it will work quite well. . . ." He takes the parchment from Shakespeare and murmurs the lines to himself, slowly at first but with growing excitement.

The sun is just coming up, and the words of one of Shakespeare's most famous soliloquies are being uttered for the first time by the first actor ever to bring Hamlet to life. It must have been an exhilarating moment.

Shakespeare wrote most of his plays to be performed live by the actor Richard Burbage and the rest of the Lord Chamberlain's men (later the King's men). Today, however, our first encounter with the plays is usually in the form of the printed word. And there is no question that reading Shakespeare for the first time isn't easy. His plays aren't comic books or magazines or the dime-store detective novels I read when I was young. A lot of his sentences are complex. Many of his words are no longer used in our everyday speech. His profound thoughts are often condensed into poetry, which is not as straightforward as prose.

Yet when you hear the words spoken aloud, a lot of the language may strike you as unexpectedly modern. For Shakespeare's plays, like any dramatic work, weren't really meant to be read; they were meant to be spoken, seen, and performed. It's amazing how lines that are so troublesome in print can flow so naturally and easily when spoken.

I think it was precisely this music that first fascinated me. When I was growing up, Shakespeare was a stranger to me. I had no particular interest in him, for I was from a different cultural tradition. It never occurred to me that his plays might be more than just something to "get through" in school, like science or math or the physical education requirement we had to fulfill. My passions then were movies, radio, and vaudeville—certainly not Elizabethan drama.

I was, however, fascinated by words and language. Because I grew up in a home where Yiddish was spoken, and English was only a second language, I was acutely sensitive to the musical sounds of different languages and had an ear for lilt and cadence and rhythm in the spoken word. And so I loved reciting poems and speeches even as a very young child. In first grade I learned lots of short nature verses. "Who has seen the wind?," one of them began. My first foray into drama was playing the role of Scrooge in Charles Dickens's *A Christmas Carol* when I was eight years old. I liked summoning all the scorn and coldness I possessed and putting them into the words, "Bah, humbug!"

From there I moved on to longer and more famous poems and other works by writers of the 1930s. Then, in junior high school, I made my first acquaintance with Shakespeare through his play *Julius Caesar*. Our teacher, Miss McKay, assigned the class a passage to memorize from the opening scene of the play, the one that begins "Wherefore rejoice? What conquest brings he home?" The passage seemed so wonderfully theatrical and alive to me, and the experience of memorizing and reciting it was so much fun, that I went on to memorize another speech from the play on my own.

I chose Mark Antony's address to the crowd in Act 3,

scene 2, which struck me then as incredibly high drama.
Even today, when I speak the words, I feel the same thrill I
did that first time. There is the strong and athletic Antony
descending from the raised pulpit where he has been speaking, right into the midst of a crowded Roman square. Holding the torn and bloody cloak of the murdered Julius
Caesar in his hand, he begins to speak to the people of
Rome:

> If you have tears, prepare to shed them now.
> You all do know this mantle. I remember
> The first time ever Caesar put it on;
> 'Twas on a summer's evening in his tent,
> That day he overcame the Nervii.
> Look, in this place ran Cassius' dagger through.
> See what a rent the envious Casca made.
> Through this the well-belovèd Brutus stabbed,
> And as he plucked his cursèd steel away,
> Mark how the blood of Caesar followed it,
> As rushing out of doors to be resolved
> If Brutus so unkindly knocked or no;
> For Brutus, as you know, was Caesar's angel.
> Judge, O you gods, how dearly Caesar loved him!
> This was the most unkindest cut of all . . .

I'm not sure now that I even knew Shakespeare had written a lot of other plays, or that he was considered "timeless," "universal," or "classic"—but I knew a good speech
when I heard one, and I found the splendid rhythms of
Antony's rhetoric as exciting as anything I'd ever come
across.

Fifty years later, I still feel that way. Hearing good actors
speak Shakespeare gracefully and naturally is a wonderful
experience, unlike any other I know. There's a satisfying
fullness to the spoken word that the printed page just can't
convey. This is why seeing the plays of Shakespeare performed live in a theater is the best way to appreciate them.
If you can't do that, listening to sound recordings or watching film versions of the plays is the next best thing.

But if you do start with the printed word, use the play as a
script. Be an actor yourself and say the lines out loud. Don't
worry too much at first about words you don't immediately
understand. Look them up in the footnotes or a dictionary,

but don't spend too much time on this. It is more profitable (and fun) to get the sense of a passage and sing it out. Speak naturally, almost as if you were talking to a friend, but be sure to enunciate the words properly. You'll be surprised at how much you understand simply by speaking the speech "trippingly on the tongue," as Hamlet advises the Players.

You might start, as I once did, with a speech from *Julius Caesar*, in which the tribune (city official) Marullus scolds the commoners for transferring their loyalties so quickly from the defeated and murdered general Pompey to the newly victorious Julius Caesar:

> Wherefore rejoice? What conquest brings he home?
> What tributaries follow him to Rome
> To grace in captive bonds his chariot wheels?
> You blocks, you stones, you worse than senseless
>   things!
> O you hard hearts, you cruel men of Rome,
> Knew you not Pompey? Many a time and oft
> Have you climbed up to walls and battlements,
> To towers and windows, yea, to chimney tops,
> Your infants in your arms, and there have sat
> The livelong day, with patient expectation,
> To see great Pompey pass the streets of Rome.

With the exception of one or two words like "wherefore" (which means "why," not "where"), "tributaries" (which means "captives"), and "patient expectation" (which means patient waiting), the meaning and emotions of this speech can be easily understood.

From here you can go on to dialogues or other more challenging scenes. Although you may stumble over unaccustomed phrases or unfamiliar words at first, and even fall flat when you're crossing some particularly rocky passages, pick yourself up and stay with it. Remember that it takes time to feel at home with anything new. Soon you'll come to recognize Shakespeare's unique sense of humor and way of saying things as easily as you recognize a friend's laughter.

And then it will just be a matter of choosing which one of Shakespeare's plays you want to tackle next. As a true fan of his, you'll find that you're constantly learning from his plays. It's a journey of discovery that you can continue for the rest of your life. For no matter how many times you read or see a particular play, there will always be something new there that you won't have noticed before.

Why do so many thousands of people get hooked on Shakespeare and develop a habit that lasts a lifetime? What can he really say to us today, in a world filled with inventions and problems he never could have imagined? And how do you get past his special language and difficult sentence structure to understand him?

The best way to answer these questions is to go see a live production. You might not know much about Shakespeare, or much about the theater, but when you watch actors performing one of his plays on the stage, it will soon become clear to you why people get so excited about a playwright who lived hundreds of years ago.

For the story—what's happening in the play—is the most accessible part of Shakespeare. In *A Midsummer Night's Dream*, for example, you can immediately understand the situation: a girl is chasing a guy who's chasing a girl who's chasing another guy. No wonder *A Midsummer Night's Dream* is one of the most popular of Shakespeare's plays: it's about one of the world's most popular pastimes— falling in love.

But the course of true love never did run smooth, as the young suitor Lysander says. Often in Shakespeare's comedies the girl whom the guy loves doesn't love him back, or she loves him but he loves someone else. In *The Two Gentlemen of Verona*, Julia loves Proteus, Proteus loves Sylvia, and Sylvia loves Valentine, who is Proteus's best friend. In the end, of course, true love prevails, but not without lots of complications along the way.

For in all of his plays—comedies, histories, and tragedies—Shakespeare is showing you human nature. His characters act and react in the most extraordinary ways—and sometimes in the most incomprehensible ways. People are always trying to find motivations for what a character does. They ask, "Why does Iago want to destroy Othello?"

The answer, to me, is very simple—because that's the way Iago is. That's just his nature. Shakespeare doesn't explain his characters; he sets them in motion—and away they go. He doesn't worry about whether they're likable or not. He's interested in interesting people, and his most fascinating characters are those who are unpredictable. If you lean back in your chair early on in one of his plays, thinking you've figured out what Iago or Shylock (in *The Merchant of Venice*) is up to, don't be too sure—because that great judge of human nature, Shakespeare, will surprise you every time.

He is just as wily in the way he structures a play. In *Macbeth*, a comic scene is suddenly introduced just after the bloodiest and most treacherous slaughter imaginable, of a guest and king by his host and subject, when in comes a drunk porter who has to go to the bathroom. Shakespeare is tickling your emotions by bringing a stand-up comic on-stage right on the heels of a savage murder.

It has taken me thirty years to understand even some of these things, and so I'm not suggesting that Shakespeare is immediately understandable. I've gotten to know him not through theory but through practice, the practice of the *living* Shakespeare—the playwright of the theater.

Of course the plays are a great achievement of dramatic literature, and they should be studied and analyzed in schools and universities. But you must always remember, when reading all the words *about* the playwright and his plays, that *Shakespeare's* words came first and that in the end there is nothing greater than a single actor on the stage speaking the lines of Shakespeare.

Everything important that I know about Shakespeare comes from the practical business of producing and directing his plays in the theater. The task of classifying, criticizing, and editing Shakespeare's printed works I happily leave to others. For me, his plays really do live on the stage, not on the page. That is what he wrote them for and that is how they are best appreciated.

Although Shakespeare lived and wrote hundreds of years ago, his name rolls off my tongue as if he were my brother. As a producer and director, I feel that there is a professional relationship between us that spans the centuries. As a human being, I feel that Shakespeare has enriched my understanding of life immeasurably. I hope you'll let him do the same for you.

❖

The real tragedy in *Romeo and Juliet* is the lack of a telephone. Throughout the play slow communications cause hairline misses, and silences are tragically misinterpreted. Juliet's cry over the dead body of Romeo—"Thy lips are warm"—gets right to the heart of the tragedy. If only she had awakened seconds earlier, he would still be alive; if only he had waited seconds longer, she would have awakened. Indeed, "if only" is so often in our thoughts as we watch or read the play that it becomes a sad refrain. The prominent role that time plays makes the tragedy seem that much more senseless and unnecessary.

Romeo and Juliet is really Juliet's play, just as *Antony and Cleopatra* belongs to Cleopatra—and both are marvelous roles for talented actresses. It is amazing that in a period of theatrical history when only men and boys occupied the stage, many of Shakespeare's greatest roles were written for women. Juliet has many of the best speeches in the play, verses rich in imagery and filled with the passion of adolescent yearning. Of course other characters have good lines; there is Mercutio's zesty "O, then, I see Queen Mab hath been with you" speech (1.4), or Romeo's distracted "Death, that hath sucked the honey of thy breath, / Hath had not power yet upon thy beauty" and "Thus with a kiss I die."

But Juliet really has the lion's share of show-stopping speeches. Waiting for word from Romeo, she says impatiently, "The clock struck nine when I did send the Nurse; / In half an hour she promised to return" (2.5). Later, she calls for night (and Romeo) to come, with verse that is absolutely exquisite—"Gallop apace, you fiery-footed steeds, / Towards Phoebus' lodging!" (3.2). And then, before she drinks the sleeping potion—"I have a faint cold fear thrills through my veins / That almost freezes up the heat of life." But the best lines that Juliet has in the entire play—certainly *my* favorites—are those she says to Romeo as he departs, in Act 2, scene 2:

> My bounty is as boundless as the sea,
> My love as deep; the more I give to thee,
> The more I have, for both are infinite.

Though they sum up the deep love that Romeo and Juliet have just vowed to each other, these lines also go beyond the immediate context to the great world outside, expressing what to me is the quintessence of love.

In the past, productions of the play have been dominated by superstar actresses who insisted that the play end with Juliet's dying words: "O happy dagger! / This is thy sheath. There rust, and let me die." Happily, this way of ending the play has gone out of fashion, and modern productions preserve the play as Shakespeare wrote it, with the final scene of reconciliation between the two warring families, a scene that is essential to rounding out the tragedy. Here we have the gathering of the Capulets and Montagues, stricken by the loss of their children, a loss that forcefully brings home the futility of their hatred.

Such endings are essential to the integrity of Shakespeare's plays; he is giving the audience time to absorb the meaning of the tragedy. The ending of *Hamlet* is a case in point. Shakespeare has Fortinbras march into the midst of the horrific chaos of death to observe Hamlet's passing with appropriate ceremony and remind us that life goes on.

Even *King Lear* does not end abruptly with this old man's tragic death, which would produce a feeling of emptiness in the audience. This is not Shakespeare's objective. Instead he knows that we need a chance to breathe and to wonder, along with loyal Kent, that Lear "hath endured so long." As Nym remarks philosophically to Bardolph in *Henry V,* "There must be conclusions."

JOSEPH PAPP

JOSEPH PAPP GRATEFULLY ACKNOWLEDGES THE HELP OF ELIZABETH KIRKLAND IN PREPARING THIS FOREWORD.

ROMEO
AND
JULIET

Introduction

Though a tragedy, *Romeo and Juliet* is in some ways more closely comparable to Shakespeare's romantic comedies than to his other tragedies. Stylistically belonging to the years 1594–1596, it is in the lyric vein of the sonnets, *A Midsummer Night's Dream*, and *The Merchant of Venice*, all from the mid 1590s. Like those plays, it uses a variety of rhyme schemes (couplets, quatrains, octets, even sonnets) and revels in punning, metaphor, and wit combat. It is separated in tone and in time from the earliest of the great tragedies, *Julius Caesar* and *Hamlet*, by almost half a decade, and, except for the experimental *Titus Andronicus*, it is the only tragedy (that is not also a history) that Shakespeare wrote in the first decade of his career—a period devoted otherwise to romantic comedy and English history.

Like many comedies, *Romeo and Juliet* is a love story, celebrating the exquisite brief joy of youthful passion. Even its tragic ending stresses the poignancy of that brief beauty, not the bitter futility of love, as in *Troilus and Cressida* or *Othello*. The tragic ending of *Romeo and Juliet* underscores the observation made by a vexed lover in *A Midsummer Night's Dream* that "The course of true love never did run smooth" (1.1.134). True love in *Romeo and Juliet*, as in *A Midsummer Night's Dream*, is destined to be crossed by differences in blood or family background, differences in age, arbitrary choices of family or friends, or uncontrollable catastrophes such as war, death, and sickness. Love is thus, as in *A Midsummer Night's Dream*, "momentary as a sound, / Swift as a shadow, short as any dream," swallowed up by darkness; "So quick bright things come to confusion" (1.1.143–149). A dominant pattern of imagery in *Romeo and Juliet* evokes a corresponding sense of suddenness and violence: fire, gunpowder, hot blood, lightning, the inconstant wind, the storm-tossed or shipwrecked vessel. Love so threatened and fragile is beautiful because it is brief. A tragic outcome therefore affirms the uniqueness and pristine quality of youthful ecstasy. The flowering and fading of a joy "too rich for use, for earth too dear" (1.5.48), does not

so much condemn the unfeeling world as welcome the mar-
tyrdom of literally dying for love.

As protagonists, Romeo and Juliet lack tragic stature by
any classical definition or in terms of the medieval convention of the Fall of Princes. The lovers are not extraordinary
except in their passionate attachment to each other. They
belong to respectable families rather than to the nobility.
They are very young, more so than most tragic protagonists
(and indeed younger than most couples marrying in England at the time the play was written; the average age for
women was between twenty-one and twenty-four, for men
between twenty-four and twenty-seven). Romeo and Juliet's
dilemma of parental opposition is of the domestic sort often found in comedy. In fact, several characters in the play
partly resemble the conventional character types of the
Latin comic playwright Plautus or of Italian neoclassical
comedy: the domineering father who insists that his daughter marry according to his choice, the unwelcome rival
wooer, the garrulous and bawdy nurse, and, of course, the
lovers. The Italian novella, to which Shakespeare often
turned for his plots, made use of these same types and paid
little attention to the classical precept that protagonists in a
tragic story ought to be persons of lofty station who are
humbled through some inner flaw, or hamartia.

The story of Romeo and Juliet goes back ultimately to the
fifth-century A.D. Greek romance of *Ephesiaca*, in which we
find the motif of the sleeping potion as a means of escaping
an unwelcome marriage. Masuccio of Salerno, in his *Il Novellino*, in 1476, combined the narrative of the heroine's
deathlike trance and seeming burial alive with that of the hero's tragic failure to receive news from the friar that she is
still alive. Luigi da Porto, in his *Historia* (c. 1530), set the
scene at Verona, provided the names of Romeo and Giulietta
for the hero and heroine, added the account of their feuding
families, the Montecchi and Cappelletti, introduced the killing of Tybalt (Theobaldo), and provided other important details. Luigi's version was followed by Matteo Bandello's
famous *Novelle* of 1554, which was translated into French by
Pierre Boaistuau (1559). The French version became the
source for Arthur Brooke's long narrative poem in English,
The Tragical History of Romeus and Juliet (1562). Brooke
mentions having seen a play on the subject, but it is doubtful

that Shakespeare either knew or made use of this old play. Brooke's poem was his chief and probably only source. Shakespeare has condensed Brooke's action from nine months to less than a week, greatly expanded the role of Mercutio, and given to the Nurse a warmth and humorous richness not found in the usual Italian duenna, or *balia*. He has also tidied up the Friar's immorality and deleted the antipapal tone. Throughout all these changes, Shakespeare retains the romantic (rather than classically tragic) conception of love overwhelmed by external obstacles.

Like the romantic comedies, *Romeo and Juliet* is often funny and bawdy. Samson and Gregory in the first scene are slapstick cowards, hiding behind the law and daring to quarrel only when reinforcements arrive. The Nurse delights us with her earthy recollections of the day she weaned Juliet: the child tasting "the wormwood on the nipple / Of my dug" (1.3.31–32), the warm Italian sun, an earthquake, the Nurse's husband telling his lame but often-repeated bawdy joke about women falling on their backs. Mercutio employs his inventive and sardonic humor to twit Romeo for lovesickness and the Nurse for her pomposity. She in turn scolds Peter and plagues Juliet (who is breathlessly awaiting news from Romeo) with a history of her back ailments. Mercutio and the Nurse are among Shakespeare's bawdiest characters. Their wry and salacious view of love contrasts with the nobly innocent and yet physically passionate love of Romeo and Juliet. Mercutio and the Nurse cannot take part in the play's denouement; one dies, misinterpreting Romeo's appeasement of Tybalt, and the other proves insensitive to Juliet's depth of feeling. Yet the play loses much of its funniness and vitality with the disappearance of these engaging companions.

The lovers, too, are at first well suited to Shakespearean romantic comedy. When we meet Romeo, he is not in love with Juliet at all, despite the play's title, but is mooning over a "hardhearted wench" (in Mercutio's words) named Rosaline. This "goddess" appropriately never appears in the play; she is almost a disembodied idea in Romeo's mind, a scornful beauty like Phoebe in *As You Like It*. Romeo's love for her is tedious and self-pitying, like that of the conventional wooer in a sonnet sequence by Francesco Petrarch or one of his imitators. Juliet, although not yet fourteen, must change all this by teaching him the nature of true love. She will have none of his shopworn clichés learned in the service of Rosaline, his flowery protestations and swearing by the moon, lest they prove to be love's perjuries. With her innocent candor she insists (like many heroines of the romantic comedies) on dispelling the mask of pretense that lovers too often show each other. "Capulet" and "Montague" are mere labels, not the inner self. Although Juliet would have been more coy, she confesses, had she known that Romeo was overhearing her, she will now "prove more true / Than those that have more coying to be strange" (2.2.100–101). She is more practical than he in assessing danger and making plans. Later she also proves herself remarkably able to bear misfortune.

The comedy of the play's first half is, of course, overshadowed by the certainty of disaster. The opening chorus plainly warns us that the lovers will die. They are "star-crossed," and speak of themselves as such. Romeo fears "Some consequence yet hanging in the stars" when he reluctantly goes to the Capulets' feast (1.4.107); after he has slain Tybalt, he cries "O, I am fortune's fool!" (3.1.135); and at the news of Juliet's supposed death he proclaims "Then I defy you, stars!" (5.1.24). Yet in what sense are Romeo and Juliet "star-crossed"? The concept is deliberately broad in this play, encompassing many factors such as hatred, bumbling, bad luck, and simple lack of awareness.

The first scene presents feuding as a major cause in the tragedy. The quarrel between the two families is so ancient that the original motives are no longer even discussed. Inspired by the "fiery" Tybalt, factionalism pursues its mindless course despite the efforts of the Prince to end it. Although the elders of both families talk of peace, they call for their swords quickly enough when a fray begins. Still, this senseless hatred does not lead to tragedy until its effects are fatally complicated through misunderstanding. With poignant irony, good intentions are repeatedly undermined by lack of knowledge. We can see why Juliet does not tell her family of her secret marriage with a presumably hated Montague, but in fact Capulet has accepted Romeo as a guest in his house, praising him as a "virtuous and well governed youth" (1.5.69). For all his dictatorial ways, and the manifest advantages he sees in marrying his daughter to an aristocrat, Capulet would never knowingly force his daughter into bigamy. Not knowing of Juliet's marriage, he and his wife can only interpret her refusal to marry Paris as caprice. Count Paris himself is a victim of this tragedy of unawareness. He is an eminently suitable wooer for Juliet, rich and nobly born, yet considerate, peace-loving, and deeply fond of Juliet (as he shows by his private and sincere grief at her tomb). Certainly he would never intentionally woo a married woman. Not knowing, he plays the unattractive role of the rival wooer and dies for it. Similarly, Mercutio cannot understand Romeo's seemingly craven behavior toward Tybalt, and so begins the duel that leads to Romeo's banishment. The final scene, with Friar Laurence's retelling of the story, allows us to see the survivors confronted with what they have all unknowingly done.

Chance, or accident, plays a role of importance equal to that of hatred and unawareness. An outbreak of the plague prevents Friar John from conveying Friar Laurence's letter to Romeo at Mantua. Friar Laurence, going hurriedly to the Capulets' tomb, arrives in time for Juliet's awakening but some minutes after Romeo has killed Paris and taken poison. Juliet awakens only moments later. The Watch comes just too late to prevent her suicide. As Friar Laurence laments, "what an unkind hour / Is guilty of this lamentable chance!" (5.3.145–146). Earlier, Capulet's decision to move the wedding date up one day has crucially affected the timing. Human miscalculation contributes also to the catastrophe: Mercutio is killed under Romeo's arm, and Friar Laurence wonders unhappily if any of his complicated plans "Miscarried by my fault" (l. 267). Character and human decision play a part in this tragedy, for Romeo should not have dueled with Tybalt no matter what the provocation. In choosing to kill Tybalt, he deliberately casts aside as "effeminate" the gentle and forgiving qualities he has learned from his love of Juliet (3.1.113), and thus is guilty of a rash and self-destructive action. To ascribe the cause of the tragedy in Aristotelian fashion to his and Juliet's impulsiveness is, however, to ignore much of the rest of the play.

Instead, the ending of the play brings a pattern out of the seeming welter of mistakes and animosities. "A greater power than we can contradict / Hath thwarted our intents," says Friar Laurence, suggesting that the seeming bad luck of the delayed letter was in fact the intent of a mysterious higher intelligence (5.3.153–154). Prince Escalus, too, finds a necessary meaning in tragic event. "See what a scourge is laid upon your hate," he admonishes the Montagues and Capulets, "That heaven finds means to kill your joys with love." Romeo and Juliet are "Poor sacrifices of our enmity" (5.3.292–304). As the Prologue had foretold, their deaths will "bury their parents' strife"; the families' feud is a stubborn evil force "Which, but their children's end, naught could remove." Order is preciously restored; the price is great, but the sacrifice nonetheless confirms a sense of a larger intention in what had appeared to be simply hatred and misfortune. Throughout the play, love and hate are interrelated opposites, yoked through the rhetorical device of oxymoron or inherent contradiction. Romeo apostrophizes "O brawling love, O loving hate" (1.1.176), and Juliet later echoes his words: "My only love sprung from my only hate" (1.5.139). This paradox expresses a conflict in humankind as in the universe itself. "Two such opposèd kings encamp them still / In man as well as herbs," says Friar Laurence, "—grace and rude will" (2.3.27–28). Hatred is a condition of our corrupted wills, of our fall from grace, and it attempts to destroy what is gracious in human beings. In this cosmic strife, love must pay the sacrifice, as Romeo and Juliet do with their lives; but because their deaths are finally perceived as the cost of so much hatred, the two families come to terms with their collective guilt and resolve henceforth to be worthy of the sacrifice.

Structurally, *Romeo and Juliet* gives considerable prominence to the feuding of the two families. Public scenes occur at key points, at beginning, middle, and end (1.1, 3.1, and 5.3), and each such scene concerns violence and its consequences. The play begins with a brawl. Tybalt is a baleful presence in Act 1, scene 1, and Act 3, scene 1, implacably bent on vengeance. The three public scenes are alike too, in that they bring into confrontation the entire families of Capulets and Montagues, who call for swords and demand reprisal from the state for what they themselves have set in motion. Prince Escalus dominates these three public scenes. He must offer judgment in each, giving the families fair warning, then exiling Romeo for Tybalt's death, and finally counseling the families on the meaning of their collective tragedy. He is a spokesman for public order ("Mercy but murders, pardoning those that kill," 3.1.196) and is indeed something of a voice of reason for the play as a whole; being a Prince, he is above the family conflict though affected by it. Onstage, his role is sometimes doubled with that of the Chorus. To him is given the final speech promising both punishment and pardon, and it is he who sums up the paradoxical interdependence of love and hate. Although the morning after the catastrophe brings with it sorrow, it also brings peace, however "glooming." Escalus is spokesman for the restored order through which the families and we are reconciled to what has occurred.

In good part, the public scenes of the play serve to frame the love plot and the increasing isolation of the separated lovers, but these public scenes have a function of their own to the extent that the tragedy has touched and altered everyone. The final tableau is not the kiss of the dying lovers but the handclasp of the reconciled fathers. The long last public ceremonial is important because, although the private catastrophe of the lovers is unalterably complete, recognition occurs only when the whole story is known by all. This recognition is not that of the protagonists, as in the Aristotelian conception of recognition, nor does it accompany a reversal of the love tragedy; that reversal has already taken place in Romeo's banishment and the lovers' deaths. This lack of correspondence with an Aristotelian definition of tragedy is not a structural flaw, but rather a manifestation of the dual focus of the tragedy on the lovers and all Verona. The city itself is a kind of protagonist, suffering through its own violence and coming at last to the sad comfort that wisdom brings.

Romeo and Juliet
in Performance

Romeo and Juliet made full and imaginative use of the Elizabethan stage for which it was written, whether at the Theatre in Moorfields, at the Curtain, or in revival (after 1599) at the Globe Theatre. The play has an unusual number of scenes that begin in one location and then shift to another before the audience's eyes, providing continuous action where more traditional staging would call for a curtain or a change of sets. For example, at the end of Act 1, scene 4, during which the stage has represented a street in Verona near Capulet's house, Mercutio and his fellow maskers (including Romeo) do not exit to end the scene, but instead *"march about the stage"* to indicate that they are proceeding to Capulet's house, and then stand to one side. Servants immediately *"come forth with napkins,"* suggesting by these props and their servants' attire, as well as by their conversation, that the scene has now shifted inside to the hall at Capulet's house. There is talk of joint stools and the "plate"; Capulet, his family, and the guests come forward to greet the maskers, and the action proceeds swiftly to the meeting of Romeo and Juliet.

After the dancing, as well, the scene moves forward almost without interruption. The stage is briefly cleared at the start of Act 2, with the departure of the evening's guests, but at once Romeo returns onstage, refusing to go home and insistent on trying to see Juliet again. When he hears his friends Mercutio and Benvolio looking for him, he hides, perhaps behind a pillar on the open Elizabethan stage, until they have left. The "orchard wall" they suspect he has leapt over certainly need not have been supplied onstage; the actor's gestures of concealment are enough to convey the idea. Once his friends have departed, Romeo comes forward, now within the "orchard" or garden; although he has not left the stage, the scene has shifted to a new location. (The conventional marking of a new scene, 2.2, is in this sense misleading.) He beholds a light in "yonder window" and then Juliet herself; she is in the gallery above and to the rear of the stage, as though at her window. The entire stage facade in the Elizabethan theater, without scenery, provides a plausible visual impression of a house and window, while Romeo, below, is clearly understood to be in the garden adjoining the house. The vertical relationship between window and garden is spatially unmistakable and theatrically significant: the lovers are separated, and Juliet is high above Romeo's head like a "bright angel" or "winged messenger of heaven." Scenery is not only unnecessary for the visual transformations of this scene, but would render them theatrically meaningless.

When Romeo bids farewell to Juliet on his way to exile (3.5), Shakespeare uses another kind of scenic flexibility permitted him by his theater. The lovers begin the scene at Juliet's window, at daybreak. Romeo descends from Juliet's window by means of a rope ladder, in full view of the audience, and is once again in Capulet's garden, once more below Juliet and separated from her by an impossible distance. After he has made his exit, however, the concluding action of Act 3, scene 5, does not remain "aloft." Juliet's mother enters to tell Juliet of her father's intention that she marry Paris. Juliet, rather than receiving her mother in what heretofore has been her chamber, that is, the upper acting area, or gallery, *"goeth down"* from her window. (This stage direction is from the so-called "bad" quarto of 1597, which is unreliable in most ways but often informative on staging, since the "reporter" who stole the text was at a performance and tells what he saw.) After a brief pause, Juliet reenters on the main stage platform, now understood to represent her chambers, and goes through the stormy scene with her father. This remainder of Act 3, scene 5, simply has too many participants and too much action to be confined in the gallery above the stage.

Later, when Juliet has taken the sleeping potion given her by the Friar, Juliet's bed provides continuity throughout a dramatic sequence conventionally broken down into three separate scenes (4.3–5). As Juliet takes the potion, the "bad" quarto tells us, she *"falls upon her bed, within the curtains,"* drawing the bed curtains in such a way as to conceal herself from the audience. The bed has either been thrust onstage, as happens not infrequently in Elizabethan plays, or is located in the "discovery space," the curtained alcove at the rear of the stage. Here Juliet lies while members of the Capulet household bustle about, noisily preparing for the wedding that will never take place. The ironic discrepancy between their happy preparations and Juliet's extremity is continually reinforced for the audience by the mute presence of the bed. When the Nurse goes to the bed curtains and finds Juliet seemingly dead, a scene of mourning follows that is once again marked by ironic discrepancy, since the audience knows that she is still alive. Conventional stage divisions would deprive this sequence of much of its ironic effect.

The play's final scene at the tomb calls for an impressively metaphorical use of the stage. The discovery space or a similar location was probably used on Shakespeare's stage to represent the Capulets' burial vault, while a trapdoor in front of it served as a symbolic rather than a practical entrance to the tomb. Any such arrangement would have the effect of reinforcing thematic repetitions visually. The tomb would recall Juliet's bed, the scene of her first apparent death; as Capulet grievingly observes, "Death is my son-in-law, Death is my heir," since Death has deflowered Juliet in her bed (4.5.37–38). The tomb's grim presence backstage would also recall Juliet's lament, as she looked down from her window and saw Romeo below her, "Methinks I see thee, now thou art so low, / As one dead in the bottom of a tomb" (3.5.55–56). The strongly vertical element in these stage images connects them with the idea of tragic fall.

Throughout most of its history onstage, producers of *Romeo and Juliet* have generally taken little advantage of Shakespeare's swift, presentational mode of staging. William Davenant presented the play at the theater in Lincoln's Inn Fields in 1662, with Thomas Betterton as Mercutio, in a production that Samuel Pepys called "the worst that ever I heard." Soon afterward the text underwent significant changes. A tragicomic version, in which Romeo and Juliet do not die after all, was sometimes substituted for Shakespeare's play. John Downes reports that the two versions alternated onstage, "tragical one day and tragic-comical another." Thomas Otway's adaptation of 1679, *Caius Marius*, imposed a neoclassic structure on the play and relocated the story of star-crossed lovers to ancient Rome. This relocation made possible a timely political commentary

as well, since the ceaseless faction of Rome could be made
to illustrate, in Otway's Tory pro-monarchist view, the folly
of both Rome's republican agitators and Restoration
England's parliamentary advocates of constitutional re-
straints and the exclusion of James Stuart from the throne.
Otway's talent for knowing what audiences wanted in his
neoclassical age was evidently acute; his version displaced
Shakespeare's text for more than sixty years. Perhaps Otway's most noteworthy contribution was to allow his dying
hero to live until the heroine awakens in the tomb, so that
the two can share their final moments on earth. This idea
appealed so greatly that it was adopted in Theophilus Cib-
ber's revival of *Romeo and Juliet* at the Little Theatre in the
Haymarket, London (1744), in David Garrick's vastly influential production at the Theatre Royal, Drury Lane, in 1748,
and in Charles Gounod's opera *Romeo et Juliette* (1867).

Garrick's version, which had run for over 450 performances by 1800 and gave *Romeo and Juliet* the distinction
of being Shakespeare's most often performed play in that
era, omitted Romeo's love for Rosaline as too great a blem-
ish on his character, increased Juliet's age to eighteen, ex-
cised some language that was considered indecorous, and
rearranged scenes to accommodate the set. As the successful run proceeded, Garrick added a splendid masquerade
dance for the meeting of the lovers in Act 1, scene 5, and a
funeral procession for the burial of Juliet at the opening of
Act 5. Like other actor-managers of his day, Garrick presumably used painted scenery mounted on movable screens
to indicate a street, a ballroom, or a bedchamber; these sets
could be shifted without great delay, but they did fix the
visual setting for any segment of action in one place and
required a curtained interval before the action could move
on to another location. The Capulets' monument in Act 5
was, to judge from a contemporary (1753) engraving by R. S.
Ravenet, an enclosed vault surrounded by trees with the
moon visible in the sky. Another contemporary illustration
of Spranger Barry and Maria Isabella Nossiter as Romeo
and Juliet at the Theatre Royal, Covent Garden, in 1753, pic-
tures Juliet on a balcony. The misnaming of the "balcony
scene" (Shakespeare mentions only a window) originates in
staging conventions of this period.

The late eighteenth and early nineteenth centuries were not particularly auspicious times for *Romeo and Juliet*. John Philip Kemble acted the play in 1788, 1789 (with his sister Sarah Siddons, in her only London appearance as Juliet), and again in 1796, but never with great success. His biographer, James Boaden, wrote that "the thoughtful strength of his features was at variance with juvenile passion." Kemble, nevertheless, admired *Romeo and Juliet* and chose it as the first play to be performed at Covent Garden after he took over its management in 1803. He cast his brother Charles and Harriet Siddons as Romeo and Juliet. Charles Kemble's debut in this successful production initiated a role he continued to play until 1828. In 1829 Charles Kemble undertook the role of Mercutio and soon became a great favorite in this part. He acted it again in 1836, with Helen Faucit making her first appearance as Juliet, and for a final time in 1840 at Covent Garden as one of four command performances for the Queen. In 1838 William Charles Macready, whose first appearance onstage was as Romeo in 1810 at Birmingham, elegantly produced the play at Covent Garden, playing Friar Laurence and leaving the title roles to James Anderson and Helen Faucit. Yet Macready, who had heralded the return of Shakespeare's text to the stage with other plays, still depended on the Garrick-Kemble version of *Romeo and Juliet* that had effectively replaced Shakespeare's play onstage. In 1841 he began work on a new production that might well have restored Shakespeare's text and for which he intended to replace the usual eighteenth- or early nineteenth-century dress employed up until his time with costumes and sets that would accurately represent the style of thirteenth-century Verona. Unfortunately, he never was able to bring these plans to fruition.

The success of many lavish Shakespearean productions in the nineteenth century created a continuing expectation for verisimilar sets, ones that could be shifted only with difficulty and necessitated a rearrangement of scenes in the play. Shakespeare's text had to be substantially cut as well, but at least what remained of it was Shakespeare's language rather than the Garrick-Kemble version that had so long prevailed in the theater. When the American actress Charlotte Cushman toured England in her "breeches" role as Romeo opposite her sister Susan's Juliet, she used authentic Renaissance dress and a cut version of Shakespeare's play. The following year Samuel Phelps produced the play at the Sadler's Wells Theatre, also with Shakespeare's text restored, and revived the play four more times during his management of the theater. (In 1859 Phelps performed his *Romeo* for Queen Victoria at Windsor Castle.) Henry Irving's revival at the Lyceum Theatre in 1882 was especially illustrative of the trend toward using a cut Shakespearean text while reveling in the spectacular elements of production. "Every line suggests a picture," he said, and Irving's production was indeed elaborately pictorial, depending on some insights for the staging of crowd scenes and other matters gleaned from Helena Modjeska's production of the previous year at the Court Theatre. Irving paid special attention to horticultural and arboricultural displays, and ended with a grand tableau of the two stricken families at the tomb. Vaulted arches, stone staircases leading down into the tomb, and ironwork grill gates created a gloomy atmosphere of death into which the moon shone with poignant effect. Mary Anderson, in 1884 at the Lyceum Theatre, gave an impression of the Piazza Dante in Verona through the use of realistic masonry, delicate architectural detail, handsome gardens, flowing Renaissance gowns, satin and brocade in profusion, and elaborate machinery by means of which houses could be transformed into gardens and cloisters into tombs. Both the Friar's cell and Juliet's chamber were, according to a contemporary account, "turned inside out in full view of the house." The love scene in Capulet's garden revealed terrace after terrace descending and receding into a distant moonlit haze.

Twentieth-century staging, beginning with a production by William Poel in 1905, in the last performance by his Elizabethan Stage Society as an organized group, has helped to free the play from the restricting requirements of nineteenth-century realistic illusion. A single permanent set for the entire performance, introduced by John Gielgud at the New Theatre in 1935 (with Laurence Olivier and Gielgud exchanging the roles of Romeo and Mercutio, Peggy Ashcroft as Juliet, and Edith Evans as the Nurse), provided something like the unlocalized stage used for Shakespeare's original performance. Peter Brook, remarking that *Romeo and Juliet* is "a play of wide spaces in which all scenery and decoration can easily become an irrelevance," gave his 1947 production at Stratford-upon-Avon a stylized set of crenellated walls with which to focus and contain the play's violent passion. At Stratford-upon-Avon in 1954, Glen Byam Shaw used a partly abstract and geometrical single set, with steps in concentric circles and a curved walkway or gallery above at the back flanked by houses on either side; the decor, including the costumes, suggested Renaissance Italy. Thrust stages in many new theaters have encouraged flexibility and presentational staging methods, as in Joseph Papp's 1968 production at New York's Delacorte Theater, featuring a set of intricate scaffolds and a runway extending into the seating area on which the scene of Juliet's window and orchard (2.2) was located.

The temptation to use gorgeous scenery (and gorgeous actresses) is understandably irresistible in film, and Franco Zeffirelli's well-known film version (1968, based on an earlier stage production at the Old Vic in 1960) makes no effort to resist. In order to achieve sensuous and intimate delight in the love scenes between Leonard Whiting and Olivia Hussey, Zeffirelli has to sacrifice the sense of distance that so separated the lovers on Shakespeare's stage; Zeffirelli's lovers show us what physical passion is like, whereas Shakespeare's lovers (Juliet played by a boy actor) were required to evoke feeling through language and eloquent delivery. Zeffirelli sought in other ways to make the play readily available to modern audiences, by conceiving of Romeo not as a sensitive Renaissance courtier but as a self-absorbed teenager in love, and by suggesting Mercutio's attachment to Romeo. Terry Hands's 1973 production at Stratford-upon-Avon carried this latter idea still further, with Mercutio a "flamboyant pervert," as one reviewer called him, angry and often drunk, whose only emotional commitment is to Romeo. The musical *West Side Story* (1957), Jerome Robbins, Stephen Sondheim, and Leonard Bernstein's adaptation of the play into the milieu of New York's Spanish Harlem, unabashedly translated Shakespeare's play into terms of modern relevance. In a similar spirit, director Ron Daniels, in a production at Stratford-upon-Avon in 1980, turned the play into a study of urban violence played out on an almost bare stage with dirty plaster walls. Two years later, seeking even more baldly to make the play's social tensions relevant, the Young Vic company, in a production at Birmingham, cast black actors as Montagues and white actors as Capulets. Michael Bogdanov's production at Stratford-upon-Avon in 1986 set the play in postwar mafioso Italy. If some of these recent experiments have at times oversimplified and sensationalized rather than clarified the tensions of Shakespeare's play, they have nonetheless revealed the continuing appeal of *Romeo and Juliet* and have offered, in many cases, theatrical realizations not far removed in spirit from the Shakespearean script.

The Playhouse

This early copy of a drawing by Johannes de Witt of the Swan Theatre in London (c. 1596), made by his friend Arend van Buchell, is the only surviving contemporary sketch of the interior of a public theater in the 1590s.

From other contemporary evidence, including the stage directions and dialogue of Elizabethan plays, we can surmise that the various public theaters where Shakespeare's plays were produced (the Theatre, the Curtain, the Globe) resembled the Swan in many important particulars, though there must have been some variations as well. The public playhouses were essentially round, or polygonal, and open to the sky, forming an acting arena approximately 70 feet in diameter; they did not have a large curtain with which to open and close a scene, such as we see today in opera and some traditional theater. A platform measuring approximately 43 feet across and 27 feet deep, referred to in the de Witt drawing as the *proscaenium*, projected into the yard, *planities sive arena*. The roof, *tectum*, above the stage and supported by two pillars, could contain machinery for ascents and descents, as were required in several of Shakespeare's late plays. Above this roof was a hut, shown in the drawing with a flag flying atop it and a trumpeter at its door announcing the performance of a play. The underside of the stage roof, called the heavens, was usually richly decorated with symbolic figures of the sun, the moon, and the constellations. The platform stage stood at a height of 5½ feet or so above the yard, providing room under the stage for underworldly effects. A trapdoor, which is not visible in this drawing, gave access to the space below.

The structure at the back of the platform (labeled *mimorum aedes*), known as the tiring-house because it was the actors' attiring (dressing) space, featured at least two doors, as shown here. Some theaters seem to have also had a discovery space, or curtained recessed alcove, perhaps between the two doors—in which Falstaff could have hidden from the sheriff (*1 Henry IV*, 2.4) or Polonius could have eavesdropped on Hamlet and his mother (*Hamlet*, 3.4). This discovery space probably gave the actors a means of access to and from the tiring-house. Curtains may also have been hung in front of the stage doors on occasion. The de Witt drawing shows a gallery above the doors that extends across the back and evidently contains spectators. On occasions when action "above" demanded the use of this space, as when Juliet appears at her "window" (*Romeo and Juliet*, 2.2 and 3.5), the gallery seems to have been used by the actors, but large scenes there were impractical.

The three-tiered auditorium is perhaps best described by Thomas Platter, a visitor to London in 1599 who saw on that occasion Shakespeare's *Julius Caesar* performed at the Globe:

> The playhouses are so constructed that they play on a raised platform, so that everyone has a good view. There are different galleries and places [*orchestra, sedilia, porticus*], however, where the seating is better and more comfortable and therefore more expensive. For whoever cares to stand below only pays one English penny, but if he wishes to sit, he enters by another door [*ingressus*] and pays another penny, while if he desires to sit in the most comfortable seats, which are cushioned, where he not only sees everything well but can also be seen, then he pays yet another English penny at another door. And during the performance food and drink are carried round the audience, so that for what one cares to pay one may also have refreshment.

Scenery was not used, though the theater building itself was handsome enough to invoke a feeling of order and hierarchy that lent itself to the splendor and pageantry onstage. Portable properties, such as thrones, stools, tables, and beds, could be carried or thrust on as needed. In the scene pictured here by de Witt, a lady on a bench, attended perhaps by her waiting-gentlewoman, receives the address of a male figure. If Shakespeare had written *Twelfth Night* by 1596 for performance at the Swan, we could imagine Malvolio appearing like this as he bows before the Countess Olivia and her gentlewoman, Maria.

ROMEO
AND
JULIET

Citizens, Maskers, Torchbearers, Guards, Servants, and
  Attendants

SCENE: *Verona: Mantua*]

The Prologue [*Enter Chorus.*]

CHORUS

Two households, both alike in dignity,   1
  In fair Verona, where we lay our scene,
From ancient grudge break to new mutiny,   3
  Where civil blood makes civil hands unclean.   4
From forth the fatal loins of these two foes
  A pair of star-crossed lovers take their life;   6
Whose misadventured piteous overthrows   7
  Doth with their death bury their parents' strife.
The fearful passage of their death-marked love,   9
  And the continuance of their parents' rage
Which, but their children's end, naught could remove,
  Is now the two hours' traffic of our stage;   12
The which if you with patient ears attend,
What here shall miss, our toil shall strive to mend.   14

                         [*Exit.*]

✙

Prologue.
1 dignity rank, status   **3 mutiny** strife, discord   **4 civil . . . civil** of civil
strife . . . citizens' (with a suggestion of "civility")   **6 star-crossed**
thwarted by destiny, by adverse stars   **7 misadventured** unlucky
9 passage progress   **12 traffic** business   **14 miss** i.e., miss the mark (in
this performance).   **our toil** the actors' efforts

1.1 *Enter Samson and Gregory, with swords and
bucklers, of the house of Capulet.*

SAMSON Gregory, on my word, we'll not carry coals. 1

GREGORY No, for then we should be colliers. 2

SAMSON I mean, an we be in choler, we'll draw. 3

GREGORY Ay, while you live, draw your neck out of
collar. 5

SAMSON I strike quickly, being moved. 6

GREGORY But thou art not quickly moved to strike. 7

SAMSON A dog of the house of Montague moves me. 8

GREGORY To move is to stir, and to be valiant is to
stand. Therefore, if thou art moved, thou runn'st away. 10

SAMSON A dog of that house shall move me to stand. I
will take the wall of any man or maid of Montague's. 12

GREGORY That shows thee a weak slave, for the weakest 13
goes to the wall. 14

SAMSON 'Tis true, and therefore women, being the
weaker vessels, are ever thrust to the wall. Therefore I 16
will push Montague's men from the wall and thrust
his maids to the wall.

GREGORY The quarrel is between our masters and us 19
their men. 20

SAMSON 'Tis all one. I will show myself a tyrant: when 21
I have fought with the men, I will be civil with the
maids—I will cut off their heads.

GREGORY The heads of the maids?

SAMSON Ay, the heads of the maids, or their maiden-
heads. Take it in what sense thou wilt. 26

1.1. Location: Verona. A public place.
s.d. bucklers small shields   **1 carry coals** i.e., endure insults   **2 colliers**
(Coal carriers were regarded as dirty and of evil repute.)   **3 an** if.
choler anger (produced by one of the four humors).   **draw** draw
swords   **5 collar** i.e., hangman's noose (with pun on *colliers* and *choler*)   **6 moved** i.e., to anger (with pun in next line)   **8 moves** incites
10 stand i.e., stand one's ground   **12 take the wall** i.e., take the cleaner
side of the walk nearest the wall, thus forcing others out into the gut-
ter   **13–14 the weakest . . . wall** (A proverb expressing the idea that the
weakest are always forced to give way.)   **16 thrust to the wall** (with
bawdy suggestion)   **19–20 between . . . men** i.e., between the males of
one household and the males of the other household; the women would
not fight   **21 one** the same   **26 what sense** whatever meaning

GREGORY   They must take it in sense that feel it.   27

SAMSON   Me they shall feel while I am able to stand, and   28
'tis known I am a pretty piece of flesh.   29

GREGORY   'Tis well thou art not fish; if thou hadst, thou   30
hadst been Poor John. Draw thy tool. Here comes of   31
the house of Montagues.

    Enter two other servingmen [Abraham and
    another].

SAMSON   My naked weapon is out. Quarrel. I will back
thee.

GREGORY   How, turn thy back and run?

SAMSON   Fear me not.   36

GREGORY   No, marry. I fear thee!

SAMSON   Let us take the law of our sides. Let them   38
begin.

GREGORY   I will frown as I pass by, and let them take it
as they list.   41

SAMSON   Nay, as they dare. I will bite my thumb at   42
them, which is disgrace to them if they bear it.

        [Samson makes taunting gestures.]

ABRAHAM   Do you bite your thumb at us, sir?

SAMSON   I do bite my thumb, sir.

ABRAHAM   Do you bite your thumb at us, sir?

SAMSON   *[Aside to Gregory]*   Is the law of our side if I
say ay?

GREGORY   *[Aside to Samson]*   No.

SAMSON   *[To Abraham]*   No, sir, I do not bite my thumb at
you, sir, but I bite my thumb, sir.

GREGORY   Do you quarrel, sir?

ABRAHAM   Quarrel, sir? No, sir.

---

27 They . . . feel it i.e., it is the maids who must receive by way of
physical sensation (*sense*) what I have to offer, because they are the ones
who can feel it   **28 stand** (With bawdy suggestion, continued in the next
few lines in *draw thy tool* and *my naked weapon is out.*)   **29–30 flesh
. . . fish** (Refers to the proverbial phrase, "neither fish nor flesh.")
31 Poor John hake salted and dried—a poor Lenten kind of food (probably with a bawdy suggestion of sexual insufficiency).   **comes of** i.e.,
come members of   **36 Fear** mistrust. (But Gregory deliberately misun-
derstands in the next line, saying in effect, No indeed, do you think I'd
be afraid of you?)   **38 take the law of** have the law on   **41 list** please
42 bite my thumb i.e., make an insulting gesture

SAMSON　But if you do, sir, I am for you. I serve as good
a man as you.
ABRAHAM　No better.
SAMSON　Well, sir.

Enter Benvolio.

GREGORY [*To Samson*]　Say "better." Here comes one of
my master's kinsmen.
SAMSON [*To Abraham*]　Yes, better, sir.
ABRAHAM　You lie.
SAMSON　Draw, if you be men. Gregory, remember thy
washing blow.　　　　　　　　　　　　*They fight.* 63
BENVOLIO　Part, fools!
Put up your swords. You know not what you do.

Enter Tybalt [with sword drawn].

TYBALT
What, art thou drawn among these heartless hinds?　　66
Turn thee, Benvolio, Look upon thy death.
BENVOLIO
I do but keep the peace. Put up thy sword,
Or manage it to part these men with me.　　　　　　69
TYBALT
What, drawn and talk of peace? I hate the word
As I hate hell, all Montagues, and thee.
Have at thee, coward!　　　　　　　　　[*They fight.*] 72

*Enter three or four Citizens with clubs or
partisans.*

CITIZENS
Clubs, bills, and partisans! Strike! Beat them down!　　73
Down with the Capulets! Down with the Montagues!　　74

Enter old Capulet in his gown, and his Wife.

CAPULET
What noise is this? Give me my long sword, ho!　　75

---

63 washing slashing with great force　**66 heartless hinds** cowardly
menials　**69 manage** use　**72 Have at thee** i.e., on guard, here I come
73 Clubs rallying cry, summoning apprentices with their clubs.　**bills**
long-handled spears with hooked blades.　**partisans** long-handled
spears　**74 s.d. gown** nightgown, dressing gown　**75 long sword** heavy,
old-fashioned sword

CAPULET'S WIFE
 A crutch, a crutch! Why call you for a sword?
CAPULET
 My sword, I say! Old Montague is come
 And flourishes his blade in spite of me.   78

  Enter old Montague and his Wife.

MONTAGUE
 Thou villain Capulet!—Hold me not; let me go.
MONTAGUE'S WIFE
 Thou shalt not stir one foot to seek a foe.

  Enter Prince Escalus, with his train.

PRINCE
 Rebellious subjects, enemies to peace,
 Profaners of this neighbor-stainèd steel—   82
 Will they not hear? What, ho! You men, you beasts,
 That quench the fire of your pernicious rage
 With purple fountains issuing from your veins, 85
 On pain of torture, from those bloody hands
 Throw your mistempered weapons to the ground 87
 And hear the sentence of your movèd prince. 88
 Three civil brawls, bred of an airy word,   89
 By thee, old Capulet, and Montague,
 Have thrice disturbed the quiet of our streets
 And made Verona's ancient citizens
 Cast by their grave-beseeming ornaments   93
 To wield old partisans, in hands as old,
 Cankered with peace, to part your cankered hate. 95
 If ever you disturb our streets again
 Your lives shall pay the forfeit of the peace. 97
 For this time all the rest depart away.
 You, Capulet, shall go along with me,

---

78 spite defiance, despite **82 Profaners . . . steel** i.e., you who profane
your weapons by staining them with neighbors' blood **85 purple** i.e.,
bloody, dark red **87 mistempered** (1) having been tempered, or hardened, to a wrong use (2) malignant, angry **88 movèd** angry **89 airy**
i.e., merely a breath, trivial **93 grave-beseeming ornaments** i.e., staffs
and other appurtenances suited to wise old age **95 Cankered . . .
cankered** corroded . . . malignant **97 Your . . . peace** i.e., death will be
the penalty for breaking the peace

And, Montague, come you this afternoon,
To know our farther pleasure in this case,
To old Freetown, our common judgment-place.   102
Once more, on pain of death, all men depart.
   Exeunt [all but Montague, Montague's Wife,
            and Benvolio].

MONTAGUE
Who set this ancient quarrel new abroach?   104
Speak, nephew, were you by when it began?   105

BENVOLIO
Here were the servants of your adversary,
And yours, close fighting ere I did approach.
I drew to part them. In the instant came
The fiery Tybalt with his sword prepared,   109
Which, as he breathed defiance to my ears,
He swung about his head and cut the winds
Who, nothing hurt withal, hissed him in scorn.   112
While we were interchanging thrusts and blows,
Came more and more, and fought on part and part   114
Till the Prince came, who parted either part.   115

MONTAGUE'S WIFE
O, where is Romeo? Saw you him today?
Right glad I am he was not at this fray.

BENVOLIO
Madam, an hour before the worshiped sun
Peered forth the golden window of the east,   119
A troubled mind drave me to walk abroad,   120
Where, underneath the grove of sycamore
That westward rooteth from this city's side,   122
So early walking did I see your son.
Towards him I made, but he was ware of me   124
And stole into the covert of the wood.   125

---

102 Freetown (Brooke's translation, in his poem *Romeus and Juliet,* of
Villa Franca, as found in the Italian story.)   **common** public   **104 set
. . . abroach** reopened this old quarrel, set it flowing   **105 by** near
109 prepared drawn, ready   **112 Who, nothing** which not at all.   **withal**
therewith.   **hissed** hissed at   **114 on part and part** on one side and the
other   **115 either part** both parties   **119 forth** from forth   **120 drave**
drove.   **abroad** outside   **122 That . . . side** that grows on the west side
of this city   **124 made** moved.   **ware** wary, aware   **125 covert** cover,
hiding place

I, measuring his affections by my own,   126
Which then most sought where most might not be
    found,   127
Being one too many by my weary self,
Pursued my humor, not pursuing his,   129
And gladly shunned who gladly fled from me.   130

MONTAGUE
Many a morning hath he there been seen,
With tears augmenting the fresh morning's dew,
Adding to clouds more clouds with his deep sighs;
But all so soon as the all-cheering sun
Should in the farthest east begin to draw
The shady curtains from Aurora's bed,   136
Away from light steals home my heavy son   137
And private in his chamber pens himself,
Shuts up his windows, locks fair daylight out,
And makes himself an artificial night.
Black and portentous must this humor prove
Unless good counsel may the cause remove.

BENVOLIO
My noble uncle, do you know the cause?

MONTAGUE
I neither know it nor can learn of him.

BENVOLIO
Have you importuned him by any means?

MONTAGUE
Both by myself and many other friends.
But he, his own affections' counselor,
Is to himself—I will not say how true,   148
But to himself so secret and so close,   149
So far from sounding and discovery,   150
As is the bud bit with an envious worm   151
Ere he can spread his sweet leaves to the air
Or dedicate his beauty to the sun.
Could we but learn from whence his sorrows grow,
We would as willingly give cure as know.

126 affections wishes, inclination   **127 Which . . . found** i.e., I who then
chiefly desired a place where I might be alone   **129 humor** mood,
whim   **130 who** him who   **136 Aurora** goddess of dawn   **137 heavy**
(1) sad (2) the opposite of *light*.   **son** (punning on *sun*, l. 134)   **148 true**
trustworthy   **149 close** concealed   **150 sounding** being fathomed (to
discover deep or inner secrets)   **151 envious** malicious

Enter Romeo.

BENVOLIO
  See where he comes. So please you, step aside.   156
  I'll know his grievance or be much denied.

MONTAGUE
  I would thou wert so happy by thy stay   158
  To hear true shrift. Come, madam, let's away.   159
                Exeunt [Montague and his Wife].

BENVOLIO
  Good morrow, cousin.

ROMEO   Is the day so young?   160

BENVOLIO
  But new struck nine.

ROMEO   Ay me! Sad hours seem long.
  Was that my father that went hence so fast?

BENVOLIO
  It was. What sadness lengthens Romeo's hours?

ROMEO
  Not having that which, having, makes them short.

BENVOLIO In love?

ROMEO Out—

BENVOLIO Of love?

ROMEO
  Out of her favor where I am in love.

BENVOLIO
  Alas, that Love, so gentle in his view,   169
  Should be so tyrannous and rough in proof!   170

ROMEO
  Alas, that Love, whose view is muffled still,   171
  Should without eyes see pathways to his will!   172
  Where shall we dine?—O me! What fray was here?
  Yet tell me not, for I have heard it all.
  Here's much to do with hate, but more with love.
  Why, then, O brawling love, O loving hate,
  O anything of nothing first create,   177
  O heavy lightness, serious vanity,
  Misshapen chaos of well-seeming forms,

---

156 So please you if you please   **158 happy** fortunate, successful
159 shrift confession   **160 cousin** kinsman   **169 his view** its appearance   **170 in proof** in reality, in experience   **171 view . . . still** sight is
blindfolded always   **172 to his will** to what he wants   **177 create** created

Feather of lead, bright smoke, cold fire, sick health,
Still-waking sleep, that is not what it is!   181
This love feel I, that feel no love in this.
Dost thou not laugh?

BENVOLIO   No, coz, I rather weep.   183

ROMEO

Good heart, at what?

BENVOLIO   At thy good heart's oppression.

ROMEO

Why, such is love's transgression.
Griefs of mine own lie heavy in my breast,
Which thou wilt propagate, to have it pressed   187
With more of thine. This love that thou hast shown   188
Doth add more grief to too much of mine own.
Love is a smoke made with the fume of sighs;
Being purged, a fire sparkling in lovers' eyes;   191
Being vexed, a sea nourished with lovers' tears.
What is it else? A madness most discreet,   193
A choking gall, and a preserving sweet.
Farewell, my coz.

BENVOLIO   Soft! I will go along.   195
An if you leave me so, you do me wrong.   196

ROMEO

Tut, I have lost myself. I am not here.
This is not Romeo; he's some other where.

BENVOLIO

Tell me in sadness, who is that you love?   199

ROMEO   What, shall I groan and tell thee?

BENVOLIO

Groan? Why, no, but sadly tell me who.   201

ROMEO

Bid a sick man in sadness make his will—
A word ill urged to one that is so ill!   203
In sadness, cousin, I do love a woman.

---

181 **Still-waking** continually awake   183 **coz** cousin, kinsman
187–188 **propagate . . . thine** increase by having it, i.e., my own grief,
oppressed or made still heavier with your grief on my account
191 **purged** i.e., of smoke   193 **discreet** judicious, prudent   195 **Soft**
i.e., wait a moment   196 **An if** if   199 **sadness** seriousness.   **is that** is it
whom   201 **sadly** seriously. (But Romeo plays on the word, and on *in
sadness*, in the sense of "sorrowfully.")   203 **A word** i.e., *sadly* or *in
sadness*—too sad a word, says Romeo, for a melancholy lover

BENVOLIO
  I aimed so near when I supposed you loved.
ROMEO
  A right good markman! And she's fair I love.   206
BENVOLIO
  A right fair mark, fair coz, is soonest hit.   207
ROMEO
  Well, in that hit you miss. She'll not be hit
  With Cupid's arrow. She hath Dian's wit,   209
  And, in strong proof of chastity well armed,   210
  From love's weak childish bow she lives unharmed.
  She will not stay the siege of loving terms,   212
  Nor bide th' encounter of assailing eyes,   213
  Nor ope her lap to saint-seducing gold.
  O, she is rich in beauty, only poor
  That when she dies, with beauty dies her store.   216
BENVOLIO
  Then she hath sworn that she will still live chaste?   217
ROMEO
  She hath, and in that sparing makes huge waste,   218
  For beauty starved with her severity   219
  Cuts beauty off from all posterity.
  She is too fair, too wise, wisely too fair,
  To merit bliss by making me despair.   222
  She hath forsworn to love, and in that vow   223
  Do I live dead that live to tell it now.
BENVOLIO
  Be ruled by me. Forget to think of her.
ROMEO
  O, teach me how I should forget to think!
BENVOLIO
  By giving liberty unto thine eyes:
  Examine other beauties.
ROMEO   'Tis the way

---

206 fair beautiful   **207 fair mark** clear, distinct target   **209 Dian** Diana,
huntress and goddess of chastity   **210 proof** armor   **212 stay** submit
to   **213 bide** abide, endure   **216 store** wealth. (She will die without
children and therefore her beauty will die with her.)   **217 still** always
218 sparing miserliness   **219 starved with** killed by   **222 To . . . despair**
i.e., earning her own salvation through chaste living while driving me to
the spiritually dangerous state of despair   **223 forsworn to** renounced,
repudiated

To call hers, exquisite, in question more.   229
These happy masks that kiss fair ladies' brows,
Being black, puts us in mind they hide the fair.
He that is strucken blind cannot forget
The precious treasure of his eyesight lost.
Show me a mistress that is passing fair: 234
What doth her beauty serve but as a note
Where I may read who passed that passing fair?   236
Farewell. Thou canst not teach me to forget.

BENVOLIO
I'll pay that doctrine, or else die in debt.   *Exeunt.* 238

✦

1.2   *Enter Capulet, County Paris, and the Clown*
    [a Servingman].

CAPULET
But Montague is bound as well as I,   1
In penalty alike, and 'tis not hard, I think,
For men so old as we to keep the peace.

PARIS
Of honorable reckoning are you both,   4
And pity 'tis you lived at odds so long.
But now, my lord, what say you to my suit?

CAPULET
But saying o'er what I have said before: 7
My child is yet a stranger in the world;
She hath not seen the change of fourteen years.
Let two more summers wither in their pride
Ere we may think her ripe to be a bride.

PARIS
Younger than she are happy mothers made.

---

229 in question more even more keenly to mind, into consideration
234 passing surpassingly   **236 passed** surpassed   **238 pay that doctrine**
i.e., give that instruction.   **die in debt** i.e., feel I've failed as a friend

1.2. Location: Verona. A street.
s.d. County Count   **1 bound** legally obligated (to keep the peace)
4 reckoning estimation, repute   **7 o'er** again

CAPULET
And too soon marred are those so early made.
The earth hath swallowed all my hopes but she;
She's the hopeful lady of my earth.   15
But woo her, gentle Paris, get her heart;
My will to her consent is but a part;
And, she agreed, within her scope of choice   18
Lies my consent and fair according voice.   19
This night I hold an old accustomed feast,   20
Whereto I have invited many a guest
Such as I love; and you among the store,   22
One more, most welcome, makes my number more.
At my poor house look to behold this night
Earth-treading stars that make dark heaven light.
Such comfort as do lusty young men feel   26
When well-appareled April on the heel   27
Of limping winter treads, even such delight
Among fresh fennel buds shall you this night   29
Inherit at my house. Hear all, all see,   30
And like her most whose merit most shall be;
Which on more view of many, mine, being one,   32
May stand in number, though in reckoning none.   33
Come, go with me. [_To the Servingman, giving a paper._]
   Go, sirrah, trudge about   34
Through fair Verona; find those persons out
Whose names are written there, and to them say,
My house and welcome on their pleasure stay.   37
                         Exit [_with Paris_].
SERVINGMAN   Find them out whose names are written
   here! It is written that the shoemaker should meddle 39

---

15 the hopeful . . . earth i.e., my heir and hope for posterity. (_Earth_
includes property and lands.)   **18 she** if she be   **19 according** agree-
ing   **20 old accustomed** traditional   **22 store** group   **26 lusty** lively
27 well-appareled newly clothed in green   **29 fennel** flowering herb
thought to have the power of awakening passion   **30 Inherit** possess
32–33 Which . . . none i.e., when you have looked over many ladies, my
daughter, being one of them, may be numerically counted among the lot
but will count for little in your _reckoning_ or estimation. (Capulet puns
on _reckoning_ in the sense of arithmetical calculating, and also on the
proverbial saying "one is no number.")   **34 sirrah** (Customary form of
address to servants.)   **37 on . . . stay** wait to serve their pleasure
39 meddle (The bawdy suggestion of sexual activity is continued in _yard_
and _pencil_, slang terms for the male sexual organ.)

with his yard and the tailor with his last, the fisher with 40
his pencil, and the painter with his nets; but I am sent 41
to find those persons whose names are here writ, 42
and can never find what names the writing person 43
hath here writ. I must to the learned.—In good time! 44

Enter Benvolio and Romeo.

BENVOLIO
  Tut, man, one fire burns out another's burning,
    One pain is lessened by another's anguish; 46
  Turn giddy, and be holp by backward turning; 47
    One desperate grief cures with another's languish. 48
  Take thou some new infection to thy eye,
  And the rank poison of the old will die. 50
ROMEO
  Your plantain leaf is excellent for that. 51
BENVOLIO
  For what, I pray thee?
ROMEO   For your broken shin.
BENVOLIO   Why, Romeo, art thou mad?
ROMEO
  Not mad, but bound more than a madman is; 54
  Shut up in prison, kept without my food,
  Whipped and tormented and—Good e'en, good fellow. 56
SERVINGMAN   God gi' good e'en. I pray, sir, can you read? 57
ROMEO
  Ay, mine own fortune in my misery.

40–41 yard, last, pencil, nets (The servingman humorously assigns
these tools of a trade to the wrong person, to suggest how useless it
is for him, an illiterate servant, to be given a written instruction.)
yard yardstick. **last** a shoemaker's form. **pencil** paint brush
42–43 find . . . find locate . . . learn   **44 In good time** i.e., here comes
help   **46 another's anguish** the anguish of another pain   **47 holp**
helped. **backward** i.e., reverse   **48 cures . . . languish** is cured by the
suffering of a second *grief* or pain   **50 rank** foul   **51 Your** i.e., the kind
of thing people talk about. **plantain leaf** herb used for cuts and abra-
sions, such as a *broken* or bleeding shin. (Romeo undercuts Benvolio's
sententiousness by taking his medical metaphor literally, as if curing
love were like curing a minor cut.)   **54 bound** (The usual treatment for
madness.)   **56 Good e'en** good evening. (Used after noon.)   **57 gi'**
give you

SERVINGMAN Perhaps you have learned it without book. 59
   But, I pray, can you read anything you see?
ROMEO
   Ay, if I know the letters and the language.
SERVINGMAN Ye say honestly. Rest you merry! [*Going.*] 62
ROMEO Stay, fellow, I can read.   *He reads the letter.*
   "Signor Martino and his wife and daughters,
   County Anselme and his beauteous sisters,
   The lady widow of Vitruvio,
   Signor Placentio and his lovely nieces,
   Mercutio and his brother Valentine,
   Mine uncle Capulet, his wife, and daughters,
   My fair niece Rosaline, and Livia,
   Signor Valentio and his cousin Tybalt,
   Lucio and the lively Helena."
   A fair assembly. Whither should they come?   73
SERVINGMAN Up.
ROMEO Whither? To supper?
SERVINGMAN To our house.
ROMEO Whose house?
SERVINGMAN My master's.
ROMEO
   Indeed, I should have asked thee that before.
SERVINGMAN Now I'll tell you without asking. My master
   is the great rich Capulet; and if you be not of the
   house of Montagues, I pray, come and crush a cup of 82
   wine. Rest you merry!   [*Exit.*]
BENVOLIO
   At this same ancient feast of Capulet's   84
   Sups the fair Rosaline whom thou so loves,
   With all the admirèd beauties of Verona.
   Go thither, and with unattainted eye   87
   Compare her face with some that I shall show,
   And I will make thee think thy swan a crow.

---

59 **without book** by memory. (The servingman takes Romeo's flowery response to his simple question as though it were the title of a
literary work; his comment also suggests that one can learn misery
without knowing how to read.)   62 **Rest you merry** i.e., farewell. (The
servingman can see he is getting nowhere.)   73 **Whither** where
82 **crush** i.e., drink   84 **ancient** customary   87 **unattainted** unbiased

ROMEO
  When the devout religion of mine eye
    Maintains such falsehood, then turn tears to fires;   91
  And these who, often drowned, could never die,   92
    Transparent heretics, be burnt for liars!   93
  One fairer than my love? The all-seeing sun
  Ne'er saw her match since first the world begun.
BENVOLIO
  Tut, you saw her fair, none else being by,
  Herself poised with herself in either eye;   97
  But in that crystal scales let there be weighed   98
  Your lady's love against some other maid
  That I will show you shining at this feast,
  And she shall scant show well that now seems best.   101
ROMEO
  I'll go along, no such sight to be shown,
  But to rejoice in splendor of mine own.   [*Exeunt.*] 103

✣

1.3   *Enter Capulet's Wife and Nurse.*

WIFE
  Nurse, where's my daughter? Call her forth to me.
NURSE
  Now, by my maidenhead at twelve year old,
  I bade her come. What, lamb! What, ladybird!   3
  God forbid. Where's this girl? What, Juliet!

    Enter Juliet.

JULIET   How now? Who calls?
NURSE   Your mother.
JULIET
  Madam, I am here. What is your will?

---

91 Maintains upholds   **92 these** i.e., these my eyes.   **drowned** i.e., in
tears   **93 Transparent** (1) self-evident (2) clear   **97 poised** weighed,
balanced   **98 crystal scales** i.e., Romeo's eyes, in which the ladies are to
be balanced and compared   **101 scant** scarcely   **103 mine own** i.e., the
sight of my own Rosaline

1.3. Location: Verona. Capulet's house.
3 What (An expression of impatience.)   **ladybird** i.e., sweetheart; also,
loose woman (used endearingly, though perhaps also with the immediate apology, "God forbid")

WIFE

This is the matter.—Nurse, give leave awhile, 　　　8
We must talk in secret.—Nurse, come back again;
I have remembered me, thou's hear our counsel. 　　10
Thou knowest my daughter's of a pretty age.

NURSE

Faith, I can tell her age unto an hour.

WIFE

She's not fourteen.

NURSE 　　　　　　I'll lay fourteen of my teeth—
And yet, to my teen be it spoken, I have but four— 　　14
She's not fourteen. How long is it now
To Lammastide?

WIFE 　　　　　　A fortnight and odd days. 　　16

NURSE

Even or odd, of all days in the year,
Come Lammas Eve at night shall she be fourteen.
Susan and she—God rest all Christian souls!— 　　19
Were of an age. Well, Susan is with God;
She was too good for me. But, as I said,
On Lammas Eve at night shall she be fourteen,
That shall she, marry, I remember it well. 　　23
'Tis since the earthquake now eleven years,
And she was weaned—I never shall forget it—
Of all the days of the year, upon that day;
For I had then laid wormwood to my dug, 　　27
Sitting in the sun under the dovehouse wall.
My lord and you were then at Mantua—
Nay, I do bear a brain! But, as I said, 　　30
When it did taste the wormwood on the nipple
Of my dug and felt it bitter, pretty fool, 　　32
To see it tetchy and fall out wi' th' dug! 　　33
"Shake," quoth the dovehouse. 'Twas no need, I trow, 　34
To bid me trudge! 　　35

---

8 give leave leave us　**10 thou's** thou shalt　**14 teen** sorrow (playing on
teen and *four* in *fourteen*)　**16 Lammastide** the days near August 1
19 Susan i.e., the Nurse's own child who has evidently died　**23 marry**
i.e., by the Virgin Mary. (A mild oath.)　**27 wormwood** (A bitter-tasting
plant used to wean the child from the *dug* or teat.)　**30 bear a brain**
maintain a keen memory　**32 fool** (A term of endearment here.)
33 tetchy fretful　**34 "Shake" . . . dovehouse** i.e., the dovehouse
shook.　**trow** believe, assure you　**35 trudge** i.e., be off quickly

And since that time it is eleven years,
For then she could stand high-lone; nay, by the rood,   37
She could have run and waddled all about.
For even the day before, she broke her brow,   39
And then my husband—God be with his soul!
'A was a merry man—took up the child.   41
"Yea," quoth he, "dost thou fall upon thy face?
Thou wilt fall backward when thou hast more wit,   43
Wilt thou not, Jule?" and, by my halidom,   44
The pretty wretch left crying and said "Ay."
To see now how a jest shall come about!   46
I warrant, an I should live a thousand years,
I never should forget it. "Wilt thou not, Jule?" quoth he,
And, pretty fool, it stinted and said "Ay."   49

WIFE
Enough of this. I pray thee, hold thy peace.

NURSE
Yes, madam. Yet I cannot choose but laugh
To think it should leave crying and say "Ay."
And yet, I warrant, it had upon its brow
A bump as big as a young cockerel's stone—   54
A perilous knock—and it cried bitterly.
"Yea," quoth my husband. "Fall'st upon thy face?
Thou wilt fall backward when thou comest to age,
Wilt thou not, Jule?" It stinted and said "Ay."

JULIET
And stint thou too, I pray thee, Nurse, say I.   59

NURSE
Peace, I have done. God mark thee to his grace!
Thou wast the prettiest babe that e'er I nursed.
An I might live to see thee married once,   62
I have my wish.

WIFE
Marry, that "marry" is the very theme
I came to talk of. Tell me, daughter Juliet,
How stands your disposition to be married?   66

---

37 high-lone on her feet, without help. **rood** cross **39 broke her brow**
bruised her forehead (by falling) **41 'A** he **43 wit** understanding
44 halidom a relic or holy thing **46 come about** come true **49 stinted**
ceased **54 cockerel's stone** young rooster's testicle **59 say I** (with a
pun on *said "Ay"* of previous line) **62 once** someday **66 disposition**
inclination

JULIET
It is an honor that I dream not of.
NURSE
An honor? Were not I thine only nurse,
I would say thou hadst sucked wisdom from thy teat.   69
WIFE
Well, think of marriage now. Younger than you
Here in Verona, ladies of esteem   71
Are made already mothers. By my count
I was your mother much upon these years   73
That you are now a maid. Thus then in brief:
The valiant Paris seeks you for his love.
NURSE
A man, young lady! Lady, such a man
As all the world—why, he's a man of wax.   77
WIFE
Verona's summer hath not such a flower.
NURSE
Nay, he's a flower, in faith, a very flower.   79
WIFE
What say you? Can you love the gentleman?
This night you shall behold him at our feast.
Read o'er the volume of young Paris' face
And find delight writ there with beauty's pen;
Examine every married lineament   84
And see how one another lends content,   85
And what obscured in this fair volume lies
Find written in the margent of his eyes.   87
This precious book of love, this unbound lover,   88
To beautify him, only lacks a cover.   89
The fish lives in the sea, and 'tis much pride   90
For fair without the fair within to hide.   91

69 thy teat i.e., the teat that nourished you   **71 esteem** worth, nobility
73 much . . . years at much the same age   **77 a man of wax** such as one
would picture in wax, i.e., handsome   **79 Nay** i.e., indeed   **84 married**
harmonized.   **lineament** facial feature   **85 content** (1) satisfaction
(2) substance   **87 margent** commentary or marginal gloss   **88 unbound**
i.e., because not bound in marriage (with a double meaning in the
continuing metaphor of an unbound book)   **89 a cover** i.e., marriage, a
wife   **90–91 The fish . . . hide** i.e., the fish has its own suitable environ-
ment, and similarly in marriage the fair Juliet (here imagined as a
beautiful book cover "binding" Paris) would suitably embrace Paris's
worth

That book in many's eyes doth share the glory   92
That in gold clasps locks in the golden story;   93
So shall you share all that he doth possess,
By having him, making yourself no less.

NURSE
No less? Nay, bigger. Women grow by men.   96

WIFE
Speak briefly: can you like of Paris' love?   97

JULIET
I'll look to like, if looking liking move,   98
But no more deep will I endart mine eye   99
Than your consent gives strength to make it fly.

    Enter Servingman.

SERVINGMAN Madam, the guests are come, supper
served up, you called, my young lady asked for, the
Nurse cursed in the pantry, and everything in extremity. 103
I must hence to wait. I beseech you, follow straight.   104

WIFE
We follow thee. [*Exit Servingman.*] Juliet, the County
stays.   105

NURSE
Go, girl, seek happy nights to happy days.   *Exeunt.*

✛

1.4   *Enter Romeo, Mercutio, Benvolio, with five or
six other maskers; torchbearers.*

ROMEO
What, shall this speech be spoke for our excuse?   1
Or shall we on without apology?   2

92–93 That book . . . story i.e., in many persons' eyes a good story is all
the more admirable for being handsomely bound.   **clasps** (1) book
fastenings (2) embraces   **96 bigger** i.e., by pregnancy   **97 like of** be
pleased with   **98 liking move** may provoke affection   **99 endart mine
eye** i.e., let my eyes shoot Love's darts   **103 cursed** i.e., for not helping
with the preparations   **104 straight** at once   **105 County stays** Count
(Paris) waits for you

1.4. Location: Verona. A street in the vicinity of Capulet's house.
1 speech (Maskers were customarily preceded by a messenger or "presenter" with a set speech of compliment.)   **2 on** go on, approach

BENVOLIO
  The date is out of such prolixity. 3
  We'll have no Cupid hoodwinked with a scarf, 4
  Bearing a Tartar's painted bow of lath, 5
  Scaring the ladies like a crowkeeper; 6
  Nor no without-book prologue, faintly spoke 7
  After the prompter, for our entrance;
  But, let them measure us by what they will,
  We'll measure them a measure, and be gone. 10

ROMEO
  Give me a torch. I am not for this ambling.
  Being but heavy, I will bear the light. 12

MERCUTIO
  Nay, gentle Romeo, we must have you dance.

ROMEO
  Not I, believe me. You have dancing shoes
  With nimble soles; I have a soul of lead
  So stakes me to the ground I cannot move.

MERCUTIO
  You are a lover; borrow Cupid's wings
  And soar with them above a common bound. 18

ROMEO
  I am too sore enpiercèd with his shaft 19
  To soar with his light feathers, and so bound 20
  I cannot bound a pitch above dull woe. 21
  Under love's heavy burden do I sink.

MERCUTIO
  And, to sink in it, should you burden love— 23
  Too great oppression for a tender thing.

3 The date ... prolixity such windy rhetoric is out of fashion. (Directors sometimes assign this speech to Mercutio.) **4 Cupid** i.e., messenger or "presenter," probably a boy, disguised as Cupid. **hoodwinked** blindfolded **5 Tartar's ... bow** (Tartar's bows, shorter and more curved than the English longbow, were thought to have resembled the old Roman bow with which Cupid was pictured.) **lath** flimsy wood **6 crowkeeper** scarecrow **7 without-book** memorized **10 measure ... measure** perform for them a dance **12 heavy** (1) sad (2) the opposite of *light* (as at 1.1.137) **18 common** ordinary. **bound** (1) leap in the dance (2) limit **19 sore** sorely (with pun on *soar;* see also pun on *soles* and *soul* in l. 15) **20 bound** confined (with play in l. 21 on the sense of "leap") **21 pitch** height. (A term from falconry for the highest point of a hawk's flight.) **23 to sink ... love** i.e., if you should sink in love, you would prove a burden to it

ROMEO
  Is love a tender thing? It is too rough,
  Too rude, too boisterous, and it pricks like thorn.
MERCUTIO
  If love be rough with you, be rough with love;
  Prick love for pricking, and you beat love down.   28
  Give me a case to put my visage in.   29
                    [*He puts on a mask.*]
  A visor for a visor! What care I   30
  What curious eye doth quote deformities?   31
  Here are the beetle brows shall blush for me.
BENVOLIO
  Come knock and enter, and no sooner in
  But every man betake him to his legs.   34
ROMEO
  A torch for me. Let wantons light of heart
  Tickle the senseless rushes with their heels,   36
  For I am proverbed with a grandsire phrase: 37
  I'll be a candle holder and look on.   38
  The game was ne'er so fair, and I am done.   39
MERCUTIO
  Tut, dun's the mouse, the constable's own word.   40
  If thou art dun, we'll draw thee from the mire
  Of—save your reverence—love, wherein thou stickest   42
  Up to the ears. Come, we burn daylight, ho!   43

28 Prick . . . down i.e., if love gets rough, fight back (but with bawdy
suggestion of *pricking* as a way to satisfy desire and cause it to sub-
side)   **29 case** mask   **30 A visor . . . visor** i.e., a mask for an ugly mask-
like face   **31 quote** take notice of   **34 to his legs** i.e., to dancing
36 senseless lacking sensation.   **rushes** (used for floor covering)
37 proverbed . . . phrase furnished with an old proverb   **38 candle
holder** i.e., onlooker. (Alludes to the proverb, "A good candle holder is a
good gamester," i.e., he who merely looks on can't get in trouble.)
39 The game . . . done (Another proverbial notion, that it is wisest to
quit when the gambling is at its best.)   **40 dun's the mouse** (A common
phrase usually taken to mean "keep still." *Dun,* gray-brown color, plays
on *done,* done for. *Dun* also alludes to a Christmas game, "Dun [the
gray-brown horse] is in the mire," in which a heavy log representing a
horse was hauled out of an imaginary mire by the players.)   **constable's
own word** (A constable might caution one to keep still; Mercutio mocks
Romeo's caution as lovesickness.)   **42 save your reverence** (An apology
for an improper expression, which Mercutio supposes "love" to be.)
43 burn daylight i.e., waste time. (But Romeo quibbles, protesting that it
is not literally daytime.)

ROMEO
  Nay, that's not so.
MERCUTIO   I mean, sir, in delay
  We waste our lights in vain, like lamps by day.
  Take our good meaning, for our judgment sits   46
  Five times in that ere once in our five wits.   47
ROMEO
  And we mean well in going to this masque,
  But 'tis no wit to go.
MERCUTIO   Why, may one ask?   49
ROMEO
  I dreamt a dream tonight.
MERCUTIO   And so did I.   50
ROMEO
  Well, what was yours?
MERCUTIO   That dreamers often lie.
ROMEO
  In bed asleep, while they do dream things true.
MERCUTIO
  O, then, I see Queen Mab hath been with you.   53
  She is the fairies' midwife, and she comes
  In shape no bigger than an agate stone   55
  On the forefinger of an alderman,   56
  Drawn with a team of little atomi   57
  Over men's noses as they lie asleep.
  Her chariot is an empty hazelnut,
  Made by the joiner squirrel or old grub,   60
  Time out o' mind the fairies' coachmakers.
  Her wagon spokes made of long spinners' legs,   62
  The cover of the wings of grasshoppers,
  Her traces of the smallest spider web,
  Her collars of the moonshine's watery beams,

46–47 Take ... wits i.e., try to understand what I intend to say, relying
on common sense rather than on the exercise of wit. (The five "wits" or
faculties were common sense, imagination, fantasy, judgment, and
reason.)   **49 wit** wisdom (playing on *wits* in l. 47; *mean* in l. 48 plays on
meaning in l. 46)   **50 tonight** last night   **53 Queen Mab** (Possibly a
name of Celtic origin for the Fairy Queen.)   **55 agate stone** (Precious
stone often carved with diminutive figures and set in a ring.)
56 alderman member of the municipal council   **57 atomi** tiny creatures
(atoms)   **60 joiner** furniture maker.   **grub** insect larva (which bores
holes in nuts)   **62 spinners'** spiders'

Her whip of cricket's bone, the lash of film,   66
Her wagoner a small gray-coated gnat,   67
Not half so big as a round little worm   68
Pricked from the lazy finger of a maid.
And in this state she gallops night by night   70
Through lovers' brains, and then they dream of love;
O'er courtiers' knees, that dream on curtsies straight;   72
O'er lawyers' fingers, who straight dream on fees;
O'er ladies' lips, who straight on kisses dream,
Which oft the angry Mab with blisters plagues
Because their breaths with sweetmeats tainted are.   76
Sometimes she gallops o'er a courtier's nose,
And then dreams he of smelling out a suit.   78
And sometimes comes she with a tithe-pig's tail   79
Tickling a parson's nose as 'a lies asleep;
Then dreams he of another benefice.   81
Sometimes she driveth o'er a soldier's neck,
And then dreams he of cutting foreign throats,
Of breaches, ambuscadoes, Spanish blades,   84
Of healths five fathom deep, and then anon   85
Drums in his ear, at which he starts and wakes,
And being thus frighted swears a prayer or two
And sleeps again. This is that very Mab
That plats the manes of horses in the night,   89
And bakes the elflocks in foul sluttish hairs,   90
Which once untangled much misfortune bodes.
This is the hag, when maids lie on their backs,
That presses them and learns them first to bear,   93

---

66 film gossamer thread **67 wagoner** chariot driver **68 worm** (Alludes
to an ancient superstition that "worms breed in the fingers of the
idle.") **70 state** pomp, dignity **72 curtsies** i.e., bows, obeisances.
straight immediately **76 sweetmeats** candies or candied preserves
78 smelling . . . suit i.e., finding a petitioner who will pay for the use of
his influence at court **79 tithe-pig** pig given to the parson in lieu of
money as the parishioner's tithing, or granting of a tenth **81 benefice**
ecclesiastical living **84 breaches** opening of gaps in fortifications.
ambuscadoes ambushes. **Spanish blades** i.e., swords from Toledo,
where the best swords were made **85 healths** toasts. **five fathom deep**
a very deep or tall drink **89 plats . . . horses** (Alludes to the familiar
superstition of "witches' stirrups," tangles in the manes of horses.)
90 elflocks tangles. (Thought superstitiously to be the work of elves,
who would seek revenge if the elflocks were untangled.) **93 learns**
teaches

Making them women of good carriage.   94
This is she—
ROMEO   Peace, peace, Mercutio, peace!
Thou talk'st of nothing.
MERCUTIO   True, I talk of dreams,
Which are the children of an idle brain,
Begot of nothing but vain fantasy,   98
Which is as thin of substance as the air,
And more inconstant than the wind, who woos
Even now the frozen bosom of the north,
And being angered, puffs away from thence,
Turning his side to the dew-dropping south.
BENVOLIO
This wind you talk of blows us from ourselves.   104
Supper is done, and we shall come too late.
ROMEO
I fear, too early; for my mind misgives   106
Some consequence yet hanging in the stars
Shall bitterly begin his fearful date   108
With this night's revels, and expire the term   109
Of a despisèd life closed in my breast
By some vile forfeit of untimely death.
But He that hath the steerage of my course
Direct my suit! On, lusty gentlemen.   113
BENVOLIO   Strike, drum.   114

> *They march about the stage,*
> *and [retire to one side].*

1.5   *Servingmen come forth with napkins.*

FIRST SERVINGMAN   Where's Potpan, that he helps not to
take away? He shift a trencher? He scrape a trencher?   2

---

94 good carriage (1) commendable deportment (2) skill in bearing the
weight of men in sexual intercourse (3) able subsequently to carry a
child   **98 vain fantasy** empty imagination   **104 from ourselves** i.e.,
from our plans   **106 misgives** fears   **108 date** appointed time
109 expire bring to an end   **113 lusty** lively   **114 drum** drummer

**1.5. Location: The action, continuous from the previous scene, is now
imaginatively transferred to a hall in Capulet's house.**
2 take away clear the table.   **trencher** wooden dish or plate

SECOND SERVINGMAN   When good manners shall lie all
in one or two men's hands, and they unwashed too,
'tis a foul thing.

FIRST SERVINGMAN   Away with the joint stools, remove 6
the court cupboard, look to the plate. Good thou, save 7
me a piece of marchpane, and, as thou loves me, let 8
the porter let in Susan Grindstone and Nell. [*Exit
Second Servingman.*] Anthony and Potpan!

[*Enter two more Servingmen.*]

THIRD SERVINGMAN   Ay, boy, ready.

FIRST SERVINGMAN   You are looked for and called for,
asked for and sought for, in the great chamber.

FOURTH SERVINGMAN   We cannot be here and there
too. Cheerly, boys! Be brisk awhile, and the longer 15
liver take all.   *Exeunt.* 16

Enter [*Capulet and family and*] *all the guests and
gentlewomen to the maskers.*

CAPULET [*To the maskers*]
Welcome, gentlemen! Ladies that have their toes
Unplagued with corns will walk a bout with you.   18
Ah, my mistresses, which of you all
Will now deny to dance? She that makes dainty,   20
She, I'll swear, hath corns. Am I come near ye now?   21
Welcome, gentlemen! I have seen the day
That I have worn a visor and could tell
A whispering tale in a fair lady's ear
Such as would please. 'Tis gone, 'tis gone, 'tis gone.
You are welcome, gentlemen! Come, musicians, play.
                        Music plays, and they dance.
A hall, a hall! Give room! And foot it, girls.   27

6 joint stools stools with joined corners made by a joiner or furniture
maker **7 court cupboard** sideboard. **plate** silverware **8 marchpane** cake made from sugar and almonds, marzipan **15–16 the longer
. . . all** (A proverb, "the survivor takes all," here used to advocate
seizing the moment of pleasure.) **18 walk a bout** dance a turn
20 makes dainty seems coyly reluctant (to dance) **21 Am . . . now** i.e.,
have I hit a sensitive point, struck home **27 A hall** i.e., clear the hall
for dancing

[*To Servingmen.*] More light, you knaves, and turn the
   tables up,   28
And quench the fire; the room is grown too hot.
[*To his cousin.*] Ah, sirrah, this unlooked-for sport comes
   well.   30
Nay, sit, nay, sit, good cousin Capulet,   31
For you and I are past our dancing days.
How long is 't now since last yourself and I
Were in a mask?
SECOND CAPULET   By 'r Lady, thirty years.
CAPULET
What, man? 'Tis not so much, 'tis not so much;
'Tis since the nuptial of Lucentio,
Come Pentecost as quickly as it will,   37
Some five-and-twenty years, and then we masked.
SECOND CAPULET
'Tis more, 'tis more. His son is elder, sir;
His son is thirty.
CAPULET   Will you tell me that?
His son was but a ward two years ago.   41
ROMEO [*To a Servingman*]
What lady's that which doth enrich the hand
Of yonder knight?
SERVINGMAN   I know not, sir.
ROMEO
O, she doth teach the torches to burn bright!
It seems she hangs upon the cheek of night
As a rich jewel in an Ethiop's ear—
Beauty too rich for use, for earth too dear!   48
So shows a snowy dove trooping with crows   49
As yonder lady o'er her fellows shows.
The measure done, I'll watch her place of stand,   51
And, touching hers, make blessèd my rude hand.   52

28 turn the tables up (Tables were probably made of hinged leaves and placed on trestles. They were put aside for dancing.) **30 unlooked-for sport** i.e., arrival of the maskers, making a dance possible **31 cousin** kinsman **37 Pentecost** seventh Sunday after Easter (and never as late as mid-July, two weeks before Lammas or August 1 when, according to 1.3.16, the play takes place; a seeming inconsistency) **41 a ward** a minor under guardianship **48 dear** precious **49 shows** appears **51 The measure done** when this dance is over. **her place of stand** where she stands **52 hers** i.e., her hand. **rude** rough

Did my heart love till now? Forswear it, sight!   53
For I ne'er saw true beauty till this night.

TYBALT

This, by his voice, should be a Montague.
Fetch me my rapier, boy. What dares the slave   56
Come hither, covered with an antic face,   57
To fleer and scorn at our solemnity?   58
Now, by the stock and honor of my kin,
To strike him dead I hold it not a sin.

CAPULET

Why, how now, kinsman? Wherefore storm you so?

TYBALT

Uncle, this is a Montague, our foe,
A villain that is hither come in spite   63
To scorn at our solemnity this night.

CAPULET

Young Romeo is it?

TYBALT   'Tis he, that villain Romeo.

CAPULET

Content thee, gentle coz, let him alone.
'A bears him like a portly gentleman,   67
And, to say truth, Verona brags of him
To be a virtuous and well governed youth.
I would not for the wealth of all this town
Here in my house do him disparagement.
Therefore be patient; take no note of him.
It is my will, the which if thou respect,
Show a fair presence and put off these frowns,
An ill-beseeming semblance for a feast.   75

TYBALT

It fits when such a villain is a guest.
I'll not endure him.

CAPULET   He shall be endured.
What, goodman boy? I say he shall. Go to!   78
Am I the master here, or you? Go to.

---

53 Forswear it deny any previous oath   **56 What** how   **57 antic face**
grotesque mask   **58 fleer** look mockingly.   **solemnity** time-honored
festivity   **63 spite** malice   **67 portly** of good deportment   **75 semblance**
facial expression   **78 goodman boy** (A belittling term for Tybalt; "Goodman" applied to one below the rank of gentleman, but still of some
substance, like a wealthy farmer.)   **Go to** (An expression of irritation.)

You'll not endure him! God shall mend my soul,
You'll make a mutiny among my guests!   81
You will set cock-a-hoop! You'll be the man!   82

TYBALT
Why, uncle, 'tis a shame.

CAPULET   Go to, go to,
You are a saucy boy. Is 't so, indeed?
This trick may chance to scathe you. I know what.   85
You must contrary me! Marry, 'tis time.—   86
Well said, my hearts!—You are a princox, go.   87
Be quiet, or—More light, more light! —For shame!
I'll make you quiet, what!—Cheerly, my hearts!

TYBALT
Patience perforce with willful choler meeting   90
Makes my flesh tremble in their different greeting.   91
I will withdraw. But this intrusion shall,
Now seeming sweet, convert to bitterest gall.   *Exit.*

ROMEO [*To Juliet*]
If I profane with my unworthiest hand   94
    This holy shrine, the gentle sin is this: 95
My lips, two blushing pilgrims, ready stand
    To smooth that rough touch with a tender kiss.

JULIET
Good pilgrim, you do wrong your hand too much,
    Which mannerly devotion shows in this;   99
For saints have hands that pilgrims' hands do touch,
    And palm to palm is holy palmers' kiss.   101

ROMEO
Have not saints lips, and holy palmers too?

JULIET
Ay, pilgrim, lips that they must use in prayer.

---

81 mutiny disturbance   **82 You . . . cock-a-hoop** i.e., you will behave
recklessly, abandon all restraint.   **be the man** play the big man
85 scathe harm.   **what** what I'm doing, or what I'll do   **86 contrary**
oppose, thwart.   **'tis time** i.e., it's time you were taught a lesson
87 Well said well done. (Said to the dancers.)   **princox** saucy boy
90 Patience perforce patience upon compulsion.   **willful choler** i.e.,
passionate anger   **91 different greeting** antagonistic opposition
94–107 (These lines are in the form of a Shakespearean sonnet; they are
followed by a quatrain.)   **95 shrine** i.e., Juliet's hand   **99 mannerly**
proper   **101 palmers** pilgrims who have been to the Holy Land and
brought back a palm (with a pun on the palm of the hand)

ROMEO
  O, then, dear saint, let lips do what hands do.
    They pray; grant thou, lest faith turn to despair. 105
JULIET
  Saints do not move, though grant for prayers' sake. 106
ROMEO
  Then move not, while my prayer's effect I take. 107
                                        [*He kisses her.*]
  Thus from my lips, by thine, my sin is purged.
JULIET
    Then have my lips the sin that they have took.
ROMEO
  Sin from my lips? O trespass sweetly urged!
    Give me my sin again.   [*He kisses her.*]
JULIET   You kiss by th' book. 111
NURSE [*Approaching*]
  Madam, your mother craves a word with you.
                                        [*Juliet retires.*]
ROMEO
  What is her mother?
NURSE   Marry, bachelor, 113
  Her mother is the lady of the house,
  And a good lady, and a wise and virtuous.
  I nursed her daughter that you talked withal. 116
  I tell you, he that can lay hold of her
  Shall have the chinks.
ROMEO   Is she a Capulet? 118
  O dear account! My life is my foe's debt. 119
BENVOLIO [*Approaching*]
  Away, begone! The sport is at the best. 120
ROMEO
  Ay, so I fear; the more is my unrest.
                          [*The maskers prepare to leave.*]

---

105 grant thou i.e., you must answer their prayers **106 move** take
the initiative. **grant** they grant (through intercession with God)
107 move (Romeo quibbles on Juliet's word in the common sense of
"change place or position.") **111 again** back again. **by th' book** i.e.,
by the rule, expertly **113 What** who. **Marry** i.e., by the Virgin Mary.
bachelor young man **116 withal** with **118 the chinks** i.e., plenty of
money **119 dear account** heavy reckoning. **my foe's debt** due to my
foe, at his mercy **120 The sport . . . best** i.e., it is time to leave. (Refers
to the proverb, "When play is at the best, it is time to leave," as at 1.4.39.)

CAPULET
Nay, gentlemen, prepare not to be gone.
We have a trifling foolish banquet towards.   123
                    [*One whispers in his ear.*]
Is it e'en so? Why, then, I thank you all.
I thank you, honest gentlemen. Good night.   125
More torches here! Come on then, let's to bed.
[*To his cousin.*] Ah, sirrah, by my fay, it waxes late.   127
I'll to my rest.
        [*All proceed to leave but Juliet and the Nurse.*]
JULIET
Come hither, Nurse. What is yond gentleman?
NURSE
The son and heir of old Tiberio.
JULIET
What's he that now is going out of door?
NURSE
Marry, that, I think, be young Petruchio.
JULIET
What's he that follows here, that would not dance?
NURSE   I know not.
JULIET
Go ask his name. [*The Nurse goes.*] If he be marrièd,
My grave is like to be my wedding bed.   136
NURSE [*Returning*]
His name is Romeo, and a Montague,
The only son of your great enemy.
JULIET
My only love sprung from my only hate!
Too early seen unknown, and known too late!
Prodigious birth of love it is to me   141
That I must love a loathèd enemy.
NURSE
What's tis? What's tis?
JULIET   A rhyme I learned even now   143
Of one I danced withal.   *One calls within* "Juliet."
NURSE   Anon, anon!   144
Come, let's away. The strangers all are gone.   *Exeunt.*

❖

123 foolish banquet towards insignificant light refreshment in prepara-
tion   **125 honest** honorable   **127 fay** faith   **136 like** likely   **141 Prodigious**
ominous   **143 tis** this. (Dialect pronunciation.)   **144 Anon** i.e., we're coming

2.0 [*Enter*] *Chorus.*

CHORUS
Now old desire doth in his deathbed lie,
   And young affection gapes to be his heir;   2
That fair for which love groaned for and would die,   3
   With tender Juliet matched, is now not fair.   4
Now Romeo is beloved and loves again,
   Alike bewitchèd by the charm of looks;   6
But to his foe supposed he must complain,   7
   And she steal love's sweet bait from fearful hooks.
Being held a foe, he may not have access
   To breathe such vows as lovers use to swear;   10
And she as much in love, her means much less
   To meet her new-belovèd anywhere.
But passion lends them power, time means, to meet,   13
Tempering extremities with extreme sweet.   [*Exit.*]   14

✣

2.1 *Enter Romeo alone.*

ROMEO
Can I go forward when my heart is here?   1
Turn back, dull earth, and find thy center out.   2
                    [*Romeo retires.*]

   Enter Benvolio with Mercutio.

BENVOLIO
Romeo! My cousin Romeo! Romeo!
MERCUTIO   He is wise
And, on my life, hath stolen him home to bed.

2.0. Chorus.
2 gapes yearns, clamors **3 fair** beauty, i.e., Rosaline **4 matched**
compared **6 Alike** i.e., equally with Juliet **7 foe supposed** i.e., Juliet, a
Capulet; also, his opposite number in the war of love. **complain** offer
his love plaint **10 use** are accustomed **13 time means** time lends them
means **14 Tempering extremities** reducing the hardships. **sweet**
sweetness, pleasure

2.1. Location: Verona. Outside of Capulet's walled orchard.
1 forward i.e., away **2 dull earth** i.e., Romeo's body. **center** i.e., Juliet.
(The figure of speech is that of humankind as a microcosm or little world.)

BENVOLIO
  He ran this way and leapt this orchard wall.
  Call, good Mercutio.
MERCUTIO   Nay, I'll conjure too.   7
  Romeo! Humors! Madman! Passion! Lover!   8
  Appear thou in the likeness of a sigh.
  Speak but one rhyme, and I am satisfied;
  Cry but "Ay me!" Pronounce but "love" and "dove."
  Speak to my gossip Venus one fair word,   12
  One nickname for her purblind son and heir,   13
  Young Abraham Cupid, he that shot so trim   14
  When King Cophetua loved the beggar maid.—   15
  He heareth not, he stirreth not, he moveth not;
  The ape is dead, and I must conjure him.—   17
  I conjure thee by Rosaline's bright eyes,
  By her high forehead and her scarlet lip,
  By her fine foot, straight leg, and quivering thigh,
  And the demesnes that there adjacent lie,   21
  That in thy likeness thou appear to us!
BENVOLIO
  An if he hear thee, thou wilt anger him.   23
MERCUTIO
  This cannot anger him. 'Twould anger him
  To raise a spirit in his mistress' circle   25
  Of some strange nature, letting it there stand   26
  Till she had laid it and conjured it down;   27
  That were some spite. My invocation   28
  Is fair and honest; in his mistress' name
  I conjure only but to raise up him.
BENVOLIO
  Come, he hath hid himself among these trees

7 conjure raise him with magical incantation   **8 Humors** moods
12 gossip crony   **13 purblind** dim-sighted   **14 Young Abraham** i.e., one
who is young and yet old, like the Biblical Abraham; Cupid was para-
doxically the youngest and oldest of the gods   **15 King Cophetua** (In an
old ballad, the King falls in love with a beggar maid and makes her his
queen.)   **17 ape** (Used as a term of endearment.)   **21 demesnes** regions
(with bawdy suggestion as to what is adjacent to the thighs; bawdy
puns on terms of conjuration continue in *raise, spirit*, i.e., phallus or
semen, *circle, stand, laid it, raise up*)   **23 An if** if   **25 circle** (1) conjuring
circle (2) vagina   **26 strange** belonging to another person (with suggestion of a rival possessing Rosaline sexually)   **27 laid it** (1) laid the spirit
to rest (2) provided sexual satisfaction leading to cessation of erection
28 were would be.   **spite** injury, vexation

To be consorted with the humorous night.   32
Blind is his love, and best befits the dark.

MERCUTIO
If love be blind, love cannot hit the mark.
Now will he sit under a medlar tree   35
And wish his mistress were that kind of fruit
As maids call medlars when they laugh alone.
O, Romeo, that she were, O, that she were
An open-arse, and thou a poppering pear!   39
Romeo, good night. I'll to my truckle bed;   40
This field bed is too cold for me to sleep.
Come, shall we go?

BENVOLIO   Go, then, for 'tis in vain
To seek him here that means not to be found.
                                   Exit [with Mercutio].

2.2

ROMEO [*Coming forward*]
He jests at scars that never felt a wound.   1
    [*A light appears above, as at Juliet's window.*]
But soft, what light through yonder window breaks?
It is the east, and Juliet is the sun.
Arise, fair sun, and kill the envious moon,
Who is already sick and pale with grief
That thou her maid art far more fair than she.   6

32 **consorted** associated.   **humorous** moist; also, influenced by humor
or mood   **35, 39 medlar, poppering** (Fruits used as slang terms for the
sexual organs, female and male respectively. The medlar was edible
only when partly decayed; the poppering pear, taking its name from
Poperinghe in Flanders, had a phallic shape; the sound of its name is
also suggestive.)   **39 open-arse** (A name for the *medlar* making explicit
the sexual metaphor.)   **40 truckle bed** a bed on casters to be rolled
under a standing bed

2.2. **Location: The action, continuous from the previous scene, is now
imaginatively transferred to inside Capulet's orchard. A rhymed couplet
links the two scenes. Romeo has been hiding from his friends as though
concealed by the orchard wall. He speaks at once, then turns to observe
Juliet's window, which is probably in the gallery above, rearstage.**
1 s.d. A light appears (Some editors assume that Juliet is visible at l. 1.)
6 maid i.e., votary of Diana, goddess of the moon and patroness of
virgins

Be not her maid, since she is envious;
Her vestal livery is but sick and green   8
And none but fools do wear it. Cast it off.
              [*Juliet is visible at her window.*]
It is my lady, O, it is my love!
O, that she knew she were!
She speaks, yet she says nothing. What of that?
Her eye discourses; I will answer it.
I am too bold. 'Tis not to me she speaks.
Two of the fairest stars in all the heaven,
Having some business, do entreat her eyes
To twinkle in their spheres till they return.   17
What if her eyes were there, they in her head?
The brightness of her cheek would shame those stars
As daylight doth a lamp; her eyes in heaven
Would through the airy region stream so bright   21
That birds would sing and think it were not night.
See how she leans her cheek upon her hand!
O, that I were a glove upon that hand,
That I might touch that cheek!

JULIET   Ay me!

ROMEO   She speaks!
O, speak again, bright angel, for thou art
As glorious to this night, being o'er my head,
As is a wingèd messenger of heaven
Unto the white-upturnèd wondering eyes   29
Of mortals that fall back to gaze on him
When he bestrides the lazy puffing clouds
And sails upon the bosom of the air.

JULIET
O Romeo, Romeo, wherefore art thou Romeo?   33
Deny thy father and refuse thy name!

---

8 Her vestal livery the uniform of Diana's chaste votaries.   **sick and green** (Suggesting the pallor of moonlight as well as anemia or *green-sickness* [see 3.5.156] to which teenage girls were susceptible.)
17 spheres transparent concentric shells supported to carry the heavenly bodies with them in their revolution around the earth   **21 stream** shine   **29 white-upturnèd** looking upward so that the whites of the eyes are visible   **33 wherefore** why

Or, if thou wilt not, be but sworn my love,
And I'll no longer be a Capulet.

ROMEO [*Aside*]

Shall I hear more, or shall I speak at this?

JULIET

'Tis but thy name that is my enemy;
Thou art thyself, though not a Montague. 39
What's Montague? It is nor hand, nor foot, 40
Nor arm, nor face, nor any other part
Belonging to a man. O, be some other name!
What's in a name? That which we call a rose
By any other word would smell as sweet;
So Romeo would, were he not Romeo called,
Retain that dear perfection which he owes 46
Without that title. Romeo, doff thy name, 47
And for thy name, which is no part of thee, 48
Take all myself.

ROMEO   I take thee at thy word!
Call me but love, and I'll be new baptized;
Henceforth I never will be Romeo.

JULIET

What man art thou that, thus bescreened in night, 52
So stumblest on my counsel?

ROMEO   By a name 53
I know not how to tell thee who I am.
My name, dear saint, is hateful to myself,
Because it is an enemy to thee;
Had I it written, I would tear the word.

JULIET

My ears have not yet drunk a hundred words
Of thy tongue's uttering, yet I know the sound:
Art thou not Romeo and a Montague?

ROMEO

Neither, fair maid, if either thee dislike. 61

JULIET

How camest thou hither, tell me, and wherefore?
The orchard walls are high and hard to climb,

---

39 though not a Montague i.e., even if you were not a Montague   **40 nor hand** neither hand   **46 owes** owns   **47 doff** cast off   **48 for** in exchange for   **52 bescreened** concealed   **53 counsel** secret thought   **61 thee dislike** displease you

And the place death, considering who thou art,
If any of my kinsmen find thee here.

ROMEO
With love's light wings did I o'erperch these walls,   66
For stony limits cannot hold love out,
And what love can do, that dares love attempt;
Therefore thy kinsmen are no stop to me.

JULIET
If they do see thee, they will murder thee.

ROMEO
Alack, there lies more peril in thine eye
Than twenty of their swords. Look thou but sweet,
And I am proof against their enmity.   73

JULIET
I would not for the world they saw thee here.

ROMEO
I have night's cloak to hide me from their eyes;
And but thou love me, let them find me here.   76
My life were better ended by their hate
Than death proroguèd, wanting of thy love.   78

JULIET
By whose direction foundst thou out this place?

ROMEO
By love, that first did prompt me to inquire.
He lent me counsel, and I lent him eyes.
I am no pilot; yet, wert thou as far
As that vast shore washed with the farthest sea,
I should adventure for such merchandise.

JULIET
Thou knowest the mask of night is on my face,
Else would a maiden blush bepaint my cheek
For that which thou hast heard me speak tonight.
Fain would I dwell on form—fain, fain deny   88
What I have spoke; but farewell compliment!   89
Dost thou love me? I know thou wilt say "Ay,"
And I will take thy word. Yet if thou swear'st
Thou mayst prove false. At lovers' perjuries,
They say, Jove laughs. O gentle Romeo,

66 o'erperch fly over   **73 proof** protected   **76 but** unless   **78 proroguèd**
postponed.   **wanting of** lacking   **88 Fain** gladly.   **dwell on form** preserve
the proper formalities   **89 compliment** etiquette, convention

If thou dost love, pronounce it faithfully.
Or if thou thinkest I am too quickly won,
I'll frown and be perverse and say thee nay,
So thou wilt woo, but else not for the world.   97
In truth, fair Montague, I am too fond,   98
And therefore thou mayst think my havior light.   99
But trust me, gentleman, I'll prove more true
Than those that have more coying to be strange.   101
I should have been more strange, I must confess,
But that thou overheardst, ere I was ware,   103
My true-love passion. Therefore pardon me,
And not impute this yielding to light love,
Which the dark night hath so discoverèd.   106

ROMEO
Lady, by yonder blessèd moon I vow,
That tips with silver all these fruit-tree tops—

JULIET
O, swear not by the moon, th' inconstant moon,
That monthly changes in her circled orb,   110
Lest that thy love prove likewise variable.

ROMEO
What shall I swear by?

JULIET   Do not swear at all;
Or, if thou wilt, swear by thy gracious self,
Which is the god of my idolatry,
And I'll believe thee.

ROMEO   If my heart's dear love—

JULIET
Well, do not swear. Although I joy in thee,
I have no joy of this contract tonight.   117
It is too rash, too unadvised, too sudden,   118
Too like the lightning, which doth cease to be
Ere one can say "It lightens." Sweet, good night!
This bud of love, by summer's ripening breath,
May prove a beauteous flower when next we meet.
Good night, good night! As sweet repose and rest   123
Come to thy heart as that within my breast!

97 So as long as, if only. else otherwise 98 fond infatuated 99 havior
light behavior frivolous 101 coying coyness. strange reserved, aloof,
modest 103 ware aware 106 Which i.e., which yielding. discoverèd
revealed 110 orb i.e., sphere; see above, l. 17 117 contract exchanging
of vows 118 unadvised unconsidered 123 As may just as

ROMEO
  O, wilt thou leave me so unsatisfied?
JULIET
  What satisfaction canst thou have tonight?
ROMEO
  Th' exchange of thy love's faithful vow for mine.
JULIET
  I gave thee mine before thou didst request it;
  And yet I would it were to give again.   129
ROMEO
  Wouldst thou withdraw it? For what purpose, love?
JULIET
  But to be frank and give it thee again.   131
  And yet I wish but for the thing I have.
  My bounty is as boundless as the sea,
  My love as deep; the more I give to thee,
  The more I have, for both are infinite.
                      [*The Nurse calls within.*]
  I hear some noise within; dear love, adieu!—
  Anon, good Nurse!—Sweet Montague, be true.
  Stay but a little, I will come again.   [*Exit, above.*]
ROMEO
  O blessèd, blessèd night! I am afeard,
  Being in night, all this is but a dream,
  Too flattering-sweet to be substantial.

    [*Enter Juliet, above.*]

JULIET
  Three words, dear Romeo, and good night indeed.
  If that thy bent of love be honorable,   143
  Thy purpose marriage, send me word tomorrow,
  By one that I'll procure to come to thee,
  Where and what time thou wilt perform the rite;
  And all my fortunes at thy foot I'll lay
  And follow thee my lord throughout the world.
NURSE [*Within*]   Madam!
JULIET
  I come, anon.—But if thou meanest not well,
  I do beseech thee—
NURSE [*Within*]   Madam!

129 were were available   **131 frank** liberal, bounteous   **143 bent** purpose

JULIET   By and by, I come—   151
  To cease thy strife and leave me to my grief.   152
  Tomorrow will I send.
ROMEO   So thrive my soul—
JULIET   A thousand times good night!   [*Exit, above.*]
ROMEO
  A thousand times the worse, to want thy light.
  Love goes toward love as schoolboys from their books,
  But love from love, toward school with heavy looks.
                        [*He starts to leave.*]
      Enter Juliet [*above*] *again.*

JULIET
  Hist! Romeo, hist! O, for a falconer's voice,
  To lure this tassel-gentle back again!   160
  Bondage is hoarse and may not speak aloud,   161
  Else would I tear the cave where Echo lies   162
  And make her airy tongue more hoarse than mine
  With repetition of "My Romeo!"
ROMEO
  It is my soul that calls upon my name.
  How silver-sweet sound lovers' tongues by night,
  Like softest music to attending ears!
JULIET
  Romeo!
ROMEO   My nyas?
JULIET   What o'clock tomorrow   168
  Shall I send to thee?
ROMEO   By the hour of nine.
JULIET
  I will not fail. 'Tis twenty years till then.—
  I have forgot why I did call thee back.
ROMEO
  Let me stand here till thou remember it.
JULIET
  I shall forget, to have thee still stand there,   173
  Remembering how I love thy company.

151 By and by immediately   **152 strife** striving   **160 tassel-gentle** tercel
gentle, the male of the goshawk   **161 Bondage is hoarse** i.e., in confine-
ment one can speak only in a loud whisper   **162 tear** pierce (with
noise).   **Echo** (In Book 3 of Ovid's *Metamorphoses*, Echo, rejected by
Narcissus, pines away in lonely caves until only her voice is left.)
168 nyas eyas, fledgling   **173 still** always

ROMEO
    And I'll still stay, to have thee still forget,
    Forgetting any other home but this.
JULIET
    'Tis almost morning. I would have thee gone—
    And yet no farther than a wanton's bird,   178
    That lets it hop a little from his hand,
    Like a poor prisoner in his twisted gyves,   180
    And with a silken thread plucks it back again,
    So loving-jealous of his liberty.   182
ROMEO
    I would I were thy bird.
JULIET   Sweet, so would I.
    Yet I should kill thee with much cherishing.
    Good night, good night! Parting is such sweet sorrow
    That I shall say good night till it be morrow.
                                        [*Exit, above.*]
ROMEO
    Sleep dwell upon thine eyes, peace in thy breast!
    Would I were sleep and peace, so sweet to rest!
    Hence will I to my ghostly friar's close cell,   189
    His help to crave, and my dear hap to tell.   *Exit.* 190

                          ✤

2.3   *Enter Friar [Laurence] alone, with a basket.*

FRIAR LAURENCE
    The gray-eyed morn smiles on the frowning night,
    Check'ring the eastern clouds with streaks of light,
    And fleckled darkness like a drunkard reels   3
    From forth day's path and Titan's fiery wheels.   4
    Now, ere the sun advance his burning eye,   5
    The day to cheer and night's dank dew to dry,
    I must up-fill this osier cage of ours   7

178 wanton's spoiled child's   **180 gyves** fetters   **182 his** its   **189 ghostly**
spiritual.   **close** narrow   **190 dear hap** good fortune

**2.3. Location: Verona. Near Friar Laurence's cell, perhaps in the monas-
tery garden.**
3 fleckled dappled   **4 From forth** out of the way of.   **Titan's** (Helios,
the sun god, was a descendant of the race of Titans.)   **5 advance** raise
7 osier cage willow basket

With baleful weeds and precious-juicèd flowers.   8
The earth that's nature's mother is her tomb;
What is her burying grave, that is her womb;
And from her womb children of divers kind
We sucking on her natural bosom find,
Many for many virtues excellent,
None but for some, and yet all different.   14
O, mickle is the powerful grace that lies   15
In plants, herbs, stones, and their true qualities.   16
For naught so vile that on the earth doth live   17
But to the earth some special good doth give;
Nor aught so good but, strained from that fair use,   19
Revolts from true birth, stumbling on abuse.
Virtue itself turns vice, being misapplied,
And vice sometime's by action dignified.

   Enter Romeo.

Within the infant rind of this weak flower
Poison hath residence and medicine power:
For this, being smelt, with that part cheers each part;   25
Being tasted, stays all senses with the heart.   26
Two such opposèd kings encamp them still   27
In man as well as herbs—grace and rude will;
And where the worser is predominant,
Full soon the canker death eats up that plant.   30

ROMEO
   Good morrow, Father.
FRIAR LAURENCE   Benedicite!   31
What early tongue so sweet saluteth me?
Young son, it argues a distempered head   33
So soon to bid good morrow to thy bed.
Care keeps his watch in every old man's eye,
And where care lodges sleep will never lie;
But where unbruisèd youth with unstuffed brain   37
Doth couch his limbs, there golden sleep doth reign.

8 baleful harmful   **14 None but for some** there are none that are not
useful for something   **15 mickle** great.   **grace** beneficent virtue
16 true proper, inherent   **17 For naught so vile** for there is nothing so
vile   **19 strained** forced, perverted   **25 that part** i.e., the odor   **26 stays**
halts   **27 still** always   **30 canker** cankerworm   **31 Benedicite** a blessing on you   **33 argues** demonstrates, provides evidence of.   **distempered** disturbed, disordered   **37 unstuffed** not overcharged, carefree

Therefore thy earliness doth me assure
Thou art uproused with some distemp'rature;
Or if not so, then here I hit it right:
Our Romeo hath not been in bed tonight.

ROMEO

That last is true. The sweeter rest was mine.

FRIAR LAURENCE

God pardon sin! Wast thou with Rosaline?

ROMEO

With Rosaline, my ghostly father? No.
I have forgot that name, and that name's woe.

FRIAR LAURENCE

That's my good son. But where hast thou been, then?

ROMEO

I'll tell thee ere thou ask it me again.
I have been feasting with mine enemy,
Where on a sudden one hath wounded me
That's by me wounded. Both our remedies   51
Within thy help and holy physic lies.   52
I bear no hatred, blessèd man, for, lo,
My intercession likewise steads my foe.   54

FRIAR LAURENCE

Be plain, good son, and homely in thy drift.   55
Riddling confession finds but riddling shrift.   56

ROMEO

Then plainly know my heart's dear love is set
On the fair daughter of rich Capulet.
As mine on hers, so hers is set on mine,
And all combined, save what thou must combine
By holy marriage. When and where and how
We met, we wooed, and made exchange of vow
I'll tell thee as we pass; but this I pray,
That thou consent to marry us today.

FRIAR LAURENCE

Holy Saint Francis, what a change is here!
Is Rosaline, that thou didst love so dear,
So soon forsaken? Young men's love then lies
Not truly in their hearts, but in their eyes.

---

51 Both our remedies i.e., the remedy for both of us   **52 physic** medicine, healing property   **54 intercession** petition.   **steads** helps
55 homely simple   **56 shrift** absolution

Jesu Maria, what a deal of brine
Hath washed thy sallow cheeks for Rosaline!   70
How much salt water thrown away in waste
To season love, that of it doth not taste!
The sun not yet thy sighs from heaven clears,
Thy old groans yet ringing in mine ancient ears.
Lo, here upon thy cheek the stain doth sit
Of an old tear that is not washed off yet.
If e'er thou wast thyself and these woes thine,   77
Thou and these woes were all for Rosaline.
And art thou changed? Pronounce this sentence then: 79
Women may fall, when there's no strength in men.

ROMEO
Thou chidst me oft for loving Rosaline.   81

FRIAR LAURENCE
For doting, not for loving, pupil mine.

ROMEO
And badst me bury love.

FRIAR LAURENCE   Not in a grave   83
To lay one in, another out to have.

ROMEO
I pray thee, chide not. She whom I love now
Doth grace for grace and love for love allow.   86
The other did not so.

FRIAR LAURENCE   O, she knew well
Thy love did read by rote, that could not spell.   88
But come, young waverer, come, go with me.
In one respect I'll thy assistant be;   90
For this alliance may so happy prove
To turn your households' rancor to pure love.   92

ROMEO
O, let us hence! I stand on sudden haste.   93

FRIAR LAURENCE
Wisely and slow. They stumble that run fast.

                             Exeunt.

❧

70 sallow sickly yellow   **77 wast thyself** i.e., were sincere   **79 sentence** sententious conclusion   **81 chidst** rebuked   **83 badst** bade   **86 grace** favor, graciousness   **88 did read by rote** i.e., repeated conventional expressions without understanding them   **90 In one respect** for one reason (at least)   **92 To** as to   **93 stand on** am in need of, insist on

2.4 *Enter Benvolio and Mercutio.*

MERCUTIO
Where the devil should this Romeo be? 1
Came he not home tonight? 2

BENVOLIO
Not to his father's. I spoke with his man.

MERCUTIO
Why, that same pale hardhearted wench, that Rosaline,
Torments him so that he will sure run mad.

BENVOLIO
Tybalt, the kinsman to old Capulet,
Hath sent a letter to his father's house.

MERCUTIO A challenge, on my life.

BENVOLIO Romeo will answer it. 9

MERCUTIO Any man that can write may answer a letter.

BENVOLIO Nay, he will answer the letter's master, how
he dares, being dared.

MERCUTIO Alas poor Romeo! He is already dead,
stabbed with a white wench's black eye, run through
the ear with a love song, the very pin of his heart cleft 15
with the blind bow-boy's butt shaft. And is he a man 16
to encounter Tybalt?

BENVOLIO Why, what is Tybalt?

MERCUTIO More than prince of cats. O, he's the 19
courageous captain of compliments. He fights as you 20
sing prick song, keeps time, distance, and pro- 21
portion; he rests his minim rests, one, two, and the 22
third in your bosom. The very butcher of a silk button, 23
a duellist, a duellist, a gentleman of the very first 24
house, of the first and second cause. Ah, the immortal 25

2.4. Location: Verona. A street.
1 should can   **2 tonight** last night   **9 answer it** accept the challenge
15 pin peg in the center of a target   **16 butt shaft** unbarbed arrow,
allotted to children and thus to Cupid   **19 prince of cats** (The name of
the king of cats in *Reynard the Fox* was Tybalt or Tybert.)   **20 captain of
compliments** master of ceremony and dueling etiquette   **21 prick song**
music written out   **21–22 proportion** rhythm   **22 minim rests** short
rests in musical notation   **23 butcher . . . button** i.e., one able to strike a
specific button on his adversary's person   **24–25 first house** best school
of fencing   **25 first and second cause** causes according to the code of
dueling that would oblige one to seek the satisfaction of one's honor

passado! The *punto reverso*! The *hay*!   26
BENVOLIO   The what?
MERCUTIO   The pox of such antic, lisping, affecting phan-   28
tasimes, these new tuners of accent! "By Jesu, a very   29
good blade! A very tall man! A very good whore!"   30
Why, is not this a lamentable thing, grandsire, that we   31
should be thus afflicted with these strange flies, these   32
fashionmongers, these pardon-me's, who stand so   33
much on the new form that they cannot sit at ease on   34
the old bench? O, their bones, their bones!   35

   Enter Romeo.

BENVOLIO   Here comes Romeo, here comes Romeo.
MERCUTIO   Without his roe, like a dried herring. O   37
flesh, flesh, how art thou fishified! Now is he for the
numbers that Petrarch flowed in. Laura to his lady was   39
but a kitchen wench—marry, she had a better love to
berhyme her—Dido a dowdy, Cleopatra a gypsy, Helen   41
and Hero hildings and harlots, Thisbe a gray eye   42
or so, but not to the purpose. Signor Romeo, *bon-*   43
jour! There's a French salutation to your French slop.   44
You gave us the counterfeit fairly last night.   45
ROMEO   Good morrow to you both. What counterfeit
did I give you?

---

26 passado forward thrust.   **punto reverso** backhanded stroke.   **hay** thrust
through. (From the Italian *hai*, meaning "you have [it].")   **28 The pox of**
plague take.   **antic** grotesque   **28–29 phantasimes** coxcombs, fantastically
dressed or mannered   **29 new tuners of accent** those who introduce new
foreign words and slang phrases into their speech   **30 tall** valiant
31 grandsire i.e., one who disapproves the new fashion and prefers old
custom   **32 flies** parasites   **33 pardon-me's** i.e., those who affect overly
polite manners.   **stand** (1) insist (2) the opposite of *sit*, l. 34   **34–35 form**
. . . **bench** (*Form* means both "fashion" or "code of manners" and
"bench.")   **35 bones** French *bon*, good (with play on English *bone*)
37 Without his roe i.e., looking thin and emaciated, sexually spent. (With a
pun on the first syllable of Romeo's name; the remaining syllables, *me-oh*,
sound like the expression of a melancholy lover. *Roe* also suggests a female
deer or "dear.")   **39 numbers** verses.   **Laura** the lady to whom the Italian
Renaissance poet Petrarch addressed his love poems. (Other romantic
heroines are named in the following passage: Dido, Queen of Carthage;
Cleopatra; Helen of Troy; Hero, beloved of Leander; and Thisbe, beloved of
Pyramus.)   **to** in comparison to   **41 dowdy** homely woman.   **gypsy** Egyp-
tian; whore   **42 hildings** good-for-nothings   **43 not** i.e., that is not
44 French slop loose trousers of French fashion   **45 fairly** handsomely,
effectively

MERCUTIO   The slip, sir, the slip. Can you not conceive?   48
ROMEO   Pardon, good Mercutio, my business was great,
  and in such a case as mine a man may strain courtesy.
MERCUTIO   That's as much as to say, such a case as yours   51
  constrains a man to bow in the hams.   52
ROMEO   Meaning, to curtsy.   53
MERCUTIO   Thou hast most kindly hit it.   54
ROMEO   A most courteous exposition.
MERCUTIO   Nay, I am the very pink of courtesy.
ROMEO   Pink for flower.
MERCUTIO   Right.
ROMEO   Why then is my pump well flowered.   59
MERCUTIO   Sure wit, follow me this jest now till thou
  hast worn out thy pump, that when the single sole of
  it is worn, the jest may remain, after the wearing, solely   62
  singular.   63
ROMEO   O single-soled jest, solely singular for the single-   64
  ness!   65
MERCUTIO   Come between us, good Benvolio. My wits
  faints.
ROMEO   Switch and spurs, switch and spurs! Or I'll cry a   68
  match.   69
MERCUTIO   Nay, if our wits run the wild-goose chase, I   70
  am done, for thou hast more of the wild goose in one
  of thy wits than, I am sure, I have in my whole five.
  Was I with you there for the goose?   73
ROMEO   Thou wast never with me for anything when
  thou wast not there for the goose.   75
MERCUTIO   I will bite thee by the ear for that jest.   76

---

48 slip (Counterfeit coins were called "slips.")   **conceive** i.e., get the joke
51 case (1) situation (2) physical condition. (Mercutio also bawdily suggests
that Romeo has been in a *case,* i.e., the female genitalia.)   **52 bow in the
hams** (1) kneel, curtsy (2) show the effects of venereal disease   **53 curtsy**
make obeisance   **54 kindly** naturally; politely   **59 pump** shoe.   **well
flowered** expertly pinked or perforated in ornamental figures   **62–63 solely
singular** unique   **64 single-soled** i.e., thin, contemptible   **64–65 singleness**
feebleness   **68 Switch and spurs** i.e., keep up the rapid pace of the hunt (in
the game of wits)   **68–69 cry a match** claim the victory   **70 wild-goose
chase** a horse race in which the leading rider dares his competitors to
follow him wherever he goes   **73 Was . . . goose** did I score a point in
calling you a goose   **75 for the goose** (1) behaving like a goose (2) looking
for a prostitute   **76 bite . . . ear** i.e., give you an affectionate nibble on the
ear. (Said ironically, however, and Romeo parries.)

ROMEO Nay, good goose, bite not.

MERCUTIO Thy wit is a very bitter sweeting; it is a most 78
sharp sauce. 79

ROMEO And is it not, then, well served in to a sweet
goose?

MERCUTIO O, here's a wit of cheveril, that stretches 82
from an inch narrow to an ell broad! 83

ROMEO I stretch it out for that word "broad," which,
added to the goose, proves thee far and wide a broad 85
goose.

MERCUTIO Why, is not this better now than groaning
for love? Now art thou sociable, now art thou Romeo;
now art thou what thou art, by art as well as by nature.
For this driveling love is like a great natural that runs 90
lolling up and down to hide his bauble in a hole. 91

BENVOLIO Stop there, stop there.

MERCUTIO Thou desirest me to stop in my tale against 93
the hair. 94

BENVOLIO Thou wouldst else have made thy tale large.

MERCUTIO O, thou art deceived; I would have made it
short, for I was come to the whole depth of my tale
and meant indeed to occupy the argument no longer.

ROMEO Here's goodly gear! 99

Enter Nurse and her man [*Peter*].

A sail, a sail!

MERCUTIO Two, two: a shirt and a smock. 101

NURSE Peter!

PETER Anon!

NURSE My fan, Peter.

MERCUTIO Good Peter, to hide her face, for her fan's the
fairer face.

---

78 sweeting sweet-flavored variety of apple **79 sharp sauce** (1) "biting"
retort (2) tart sauce, of the sort that should be served with cooked goose
(as Romeo points out) **82 cheveril** kid leather, easily stretched **83 ell**
(forty-five inches) **85 broad** large, complete; perhaps also wanton
90 natural idiot **91 lolling** with his tongue (or bauble) hanging out.
bauble (1) jester's wand (2) phallus **93–94 against the hair** against the
grain, against my wish (with a bawdy play on *tale, tail;* continued with
large, short, depth, occupy, etc.) **99 gear** substance, stuff (with sexual
innuendo) **101 a shirt . . . smock** i.e., a man and a woman

NURSE God gi' good morrow, gentlemen.

MERCUTIO God gi' good e'en, fair gentlewoman.

NURSE Is it good e'en?   109

MERCUTIO 'Tis no less, I tell ye, for the bawdy hand of
the dial is now upon the prick of noon.   111

NURSE Out upon you! What a man are you?   112

ROMEO One, gentlewoman, that God hath made for
himself to mar.   114

NURSE By my troth, it is well said. "For himself to mar,"   115
quoth 'a? Gentlemen, can any of you tell me where I   116
may find the young Romeo?

ROMEO I can tell you; but young Romeo will be older
when you have found him than he was when you
sought him. I am the youngest of that name, for fault   120
of a worse.

NURSE You say well.

MERCUTIO Yea, is the worst well? Very well took, i'   123
faith, wisely, wisely.

NURSE If you be he, sir, I desire some confidence   125
with you.

BENVOLIO She will indite him to some supper.   127

MERCUTIO A bawd, a bawd, a bawd! So ho!   128

ROMEO What hast thou found?

MERCUTIO No hare, sir, unless a hare, sir, in a lenten   130
pie, that is something stale and hoar ere it be spent.   131

[*He sings.*]

> An old hare hoar,
> And an old hare hoar,
> Is very good meat in Lent.
> But a hare that is hoar

---

109 Is it good e'en is it afternoon already   **111 prick** point on the dial
of a clock (with bawdy suggestion)   **112 Out upon you** (Expression of
indignation.)   **What** what kind of   **114 mar** i.e., disfigure morally
through sin. (Man, made in God's image, mars that image sinfully.)
115 troth faith   **116 quoth 'a** said he. (A sarcastic interjection, meaning
"forsooth" or "indeed.")   **120 fault** lack   **123 took** understood
125 confidence (The Nurse's mistake for *conference*.)   **127 indite** (Benvolio's deliberate malapropism for *invite*.)   **128 So ho** (Cry of hunter
sighting game.)   **130 hare** (Slang word for "prostitute"; similarly with
stale and *meat* in the following lines.)   **130–131 a lenten pie** a pie that
should contain no meat, in observance of Lent   **131 hoar** moldy (with
pun on *whore*).   **spent** consumed

Is too much for a score,   136
     When it hoars ere it be spent.
Romeo, will you come to your father's? We'll to dinner
thither.

ROMEO I will follow you.

MERCUTIO Farewell, ancient lady. Farewell, [*Singing*]
"Lady, lady, lady."   *Exeunt* [*Mercutio and Benvolio*]. 142

NURSE I pray you, sir, what saucy merchant was this 143
that was so full of his ropery?   144

ROMEO A gentleman, Nurse, that loves to hear himself
talk, and will speak more in a minute than he will
stand to in a month.   147

NURSE An 'a speak anything against me, I'll take him 148
down, an 'a were lustier than he is, and twenty such 149
Jacks; and if I cannot, I'll find those that shall. Scurvy 150
knave! I am none of his flirt-gills. I am none of his 151
skains-mates. [*To Peter.*] And thou must stand by, too, 152
and suffer every knave to use me at his pleasure!

PETER I saw no man use you at his pleasure. If I had,
my weapon should quickly have been out; I warrant 155
you, I dare draw as soon as another man, if I see occasion in a good quarrel, and the law on my side.

NURSE Now, afore God, I am so vexed that every part 158
about me quivers. Scurvy knave! Pray you, sir, a 159
word; and as I told you, my young lady bid me inquire you out. What she bid me say, I will keep to
myself. But first let me tell ye, if ye should lead her in
a fool's paradise, as they say, it were a very gross kind
of behavior, as they say. For the gentlewoman is
young; and therefore if you should deal double with
her, truly it were an ill thing to be offered to any gentlewoman, and very weak dealing.   167

---

136 for a score for a reckoning, to pay good money for   **142 "Lady,
lady, lady"** (Refrain from the ballad *Chaste Susanna*.)   **143 merchant**
i.e., fellow   **144 ropery** vulgar humor, knavery   **147 stand to** perform,
abide by   **148–149 take him down** i.e., cut him down to size (with
unintended bawdy suggestion)   **150 Jacks** (used as a term of disparagement)   **151 flirt-gills** loose women   **152 skains-mates** (Perhaps dagger-
mates, outlaws, or gangster molls.)   **155 weapon** (with bawdy
suggestion, perhaps unrecognized by the speaker, as also in *at his
pleasure*)   **158–159 every part . . . quivers** (More bawdy suggestion,
unrecognized by the Nurse.)   **167 weak** contemptible

ROMEO Nurse, commend me to thy lady and mistress.
I protest unto thee—   169
NURSE Good heart, and i' faith I will tell her as much.
Lord, Lord, she will be a joyful woman.
ROMEO What wilt thou tell her, Nurse? Thou dost not
mark me.   173
NURSE I will tell her, sir, that you do protest, which, as
I take it, is a gentlemanlike offer.
ROMEO Bid her devise
Some means to come to shrift this afternoon,   177
And there she shall at Friar Laurence' cell
Be shrived and married. Here is for thy pains.   179
                                        [*He offers money.*]
NURSE No, truly, sir, not a penny.
ROMEO Go to, I say you shall.
NURSE
This afternoon, sir? Well, she shall be there.
ROMEO
And stay, good Nurse, behind the abbey wall.
Within this hour my man shall be with thee
And bring thee cords made like a tackled stair,   185
Which to the high topgallant of my joy   186
Must be my convoy in the secret night.   187
Farewell. Be trusty, and I'll quit thy pains.   188
Farewell. Commend me to thy mistress.
                                        [*Romeo starts to leave.*]
NURSE
Now God in heaven bless thee! Hark you, sir.
ROMEO What sayst thou, my dear Nurse?
NURSE
Is your man secret? Did you ne'er hear say,   192
"Two may keep counsel, putting one away"?   193
ROMEO
'Warrant thee, my man's as true as steel.

---

169 protest vow. (Romeo may intend only to protest his good intentions,
but the Nurse seemingly takes the word to signify a *gentlemanlike offer*
[l. 175] of marriage that would ensure against Juliet's being led into a
fool's paradise [l. 163]—i.e., being seduced.) **173 mark** attend to
177 shrift confession and absolution **179 shrived** absolved **185 tackled
stair** rope ladder **186 topgallant** highest mast and sail of a ship, the
summit **187 convoy** conveyance, means of passage **188 quit** reward,
requite **192 secret** trustworthy **193 keep counsel** keep a secret

NURSE Well, sir, my mistress is the sweetest lady—
  Lord, Lord! When 'twas a little prating thing—O,
  there is a nobleman in town, one Paris, that would
  fain lay knife aboard; but she, good soul, had as lief 198
  see a toad, a very toad, as see him. I anger her sometimes and tell her that Paris is the properer man, but 200
  I'll warrant you, when I say so, she looks as pale as
  any clout in the versal world. Doth not rosemary and 202
  Romeo begin both with a letter?   203
ROMEO Ay, Nurse, what of that? Both with an R.
NURSE Ah, mocker! That's the dog's name; R is for 205
  the—No; I know it begins with some other letter; 206
  and she hath the prettiest sententious of it, of you and 207
  rosemary, that it would do you good to hear it.
ROMEO Commend me to thy lady.
NURSE Ay, a thousand times. [*Exit Romeo.*] Peter!
PETER Anon!
NURSE Before, and apace.   *Exeunt.* 212

♣

2.5 *Enter Juliet.*

JULIET
  The clock struck nine when I did send the Nurse;
  In half an hour she promised to return.
  Perchance she cannot meet him. That's not so.
  O, she is lame! Love's heralds should be thoughts,
  Which ten times faster glide than the sun's beams
  Driving back shadows over louring hills.   6

198 **fain** gladly. **lay knife aboard** i.e., assert his claim (just as a guest
did by bringing his knife to the dinner table; with sexual suggestion
also). **lief** willingly **200 properer** handsomer **202 clout** rag, cloth.
versal universal **203 a letter** one and the same letter **205 the dog's
name** (The letter *R* was thought to resemble the dog's growl.) **206 No
. . . other letter** (The Nurse perhaps thinks that the letter means "arse"
and repudiates the association.) **207 sententious** (The Nurse probably
means *sentences*, pithy sayings.) **212 Before, and apace** go before me
quickly

**2.5. Location: Verona. Outside Capulet's house, perhaps in the orchard
or garden.**
6 louring threatening

Therefore do nimble-pinioned doves draw Love,   7
And therefore hath the wind-swift Cupid wings.
Now is the sun upon the highmost hill
Of this day's journey, and from nine till twelve
Is three long hours, yet she is not come.
Had she affections and warm youthful blood,
She would be as swift in motion as a ball;
My words would bandy her to my sweet love,   14
And his to me.
But old folks, many feign as they were dead—   16
Unwieldy, slow, heavy, and pale as lead.

     Enter Nurse [and Peter].

O God, she comes!—O honey Nurse, what news?
Hast thou met with him? Send thy man away.
NURSE   Peter, stay at the gate.   [*Exit Peter.*]
JULIET
Now, good sweet Nurse—O Lord, why lookest thou sad?
Though news be sad, yet tell them merrily;
If good, thou shamest the music of sweet news
By playing it to me with so sour a face.
NURSE
I am aweary. Give me leave awhile.   25
Fie, how my bones ache! What a jaunce have I had!   26
JULIET
I would thou hadst my bones, and I thy news.
Nay, come, I pray thee, speak. Good, good Nurse, speak.
NURSE
Jesu, what haste! Can you not stay awhile?   29
Do you not see that I am out of breath?
JULIET
How art thou out of breath, when thou hast breath
To say to me that thou art out of breath?
The excuse that thou dost make in this delay
Is longer than the tale thou dost excuse.
Is thy news good or bad? Answer to that;
Say either, and I'll stay the circumstance.   36
Let me be satisfied; is 't good or bad?

---

7 Love i.e., Venus, whose chariot was drawn by swift-winged doves
14 bandy toss to and fro, as in tennis   **16 feign as** act as though
25 Give me leave let me alone   **26 jaunce** jouncing, jolting   **29 stay**
wait   **36 stay the circumstance** await the details

NURSE Well, you have made a simple choice. You know 38
    not how to choose a man. Romeo? No, not he. Though
    his face be better than any man's, yet his leg excels all
    men's; and for a hand, and a foot, and a body, though
    they be not to be talked on, yet they are past compare. 42
    He is not the flower of courtesy, but, I'll warrant him,
    as gentle as a lamb. Go thy ways, wench. Serve God.
    What, have you dined at home?

JULIET
    No, no; but all this did I know before.
    What says he of our marriage? What of that?

NURSE
    Lord, how my head aches! What a head have I!
    It beats as it would fall in twenty pieces.
    My back o' t'other side—ah, my back, my back! 50
    Beshrew your heart for sending me about 51
    To catch my death with jauncing up and down!

JULIET
    I' faith, I am sorry that thou art not well.
    Sweet, sweet, sweet Nurse, tell me, what says my love?

NURSE
    Your love says, like an honest gentleman,
    And a courteous, and a kind, and a handsome,
    And, I warrant, a virtuous—Where is your mother?

JULIET
    Where is my mother? Why, she is within,
    Where should she be? How oddly thou repliest!
    "Your love says, like an honest gentleman,
    'Where is your mother?'"

NURSE   O God's Lady dear!
    Are you so hot? Marry, come up, I trow. 62
    Is this the poultice for my aching bones?
    Henceforward do your messages yourself.

JULIET
    Here's such a coil! Come, what says Romeo? 65

NURSE
    Have you got leave to go to shrift today?

38 simple foolish **42 be not to be talked on** are not worth discussing
(perhaps with a suggestion of being unmentionable in refined ladylike
company) **50 o' t'other** on the other **51 Beshrew** a curse on (used as a
mild oath) **62 hot** impatient. **Marry, come up** (An expression of
impatient reproof.) **65 coil** turmoil, fuss

JULIET   I have.

NURSE

Then hie you hence to Friar Laurence' cell;   68
There stays a husband to make you a wife.
Now comes the wanton blood up in your cheeks;
They'll be in scarlet straight at any news.   71
Hie you to church. I must another way,
To fetch a ladder, by the which your love
Must climb a bird's nest soon when it is dark.   74
I am the drudge, and toil in your delight,
But you shall bear the burden soon at night.
Go. I'll to dinner. Hie you to the cell.

JULIET

Hie to high fortune! Honest Nurse, farewell.

                          Exeunt [separately].

❖

2.6   *Enter Friar [Laurence] and Romeo.*

FRIAR LAURENCE

So smile the heavens upon this holy act   1
That after-hours with sorrow chide us not!

ROMEO

Amen, amen! But come what sorrow can,
It cannot countervail the exchange of joy   4
That one short minute gives me in her sight.
Do thou but close our hands with holy words,   6
Then love-devouring death do what he dare;
It is enough I may but call her mine.

FRIAR LAURENCE

These violent delights have violent ends
And in their triumph die, like fire and powder,   10
Which as they kiss consume. The sweetest honey
Is loathsome in his own deliciousness,   12

---

68 hie hasten   **71 in scarlet straight** i.e., blushing immediately
74 bird's nest i.e., Juliet's room (with suggestion of pubic hair; the
bawdry is continued in *bear the burden* two lines later)

2.6. Location: Verona. Friar Laurence's cell.
1 So . . . heavens may the heavens so smile   **4 countervail** outweigh,
counterbalance   **6 close** join   **10 powder** gunpowder   **12 his** its

And in the taste confounds the appetite.   13
Therefore love moderately. Long love doth so;
Too swift arrives as tardy as too slow.
    Enter Juliet.
Here comes the lady. O, so light a foot
Will ne'er wear out the everlasting flint.
A lover may bestride the gossamer   18
That idles in the wanton summer air,   19
And yet not fall; so light is vanity.   20

JULIET
Good even to my ghostly confessor.   21

FRIAR LAURENCE
Romeo shall thank thee, daughter, for us both.   22

JULIET
As much to him, else is his thanks too much.   23

ROMEO
Ah, Juliet, if the measure of thy joy
Be heaped like mine, and that thy skill be more   25
To blazon it, then sweeten with thy breath   26
This neighbor air, and let rich music's tongue
Unfold the imagined happiness that both   28
Receive in either by this dear encounter.   29

JULIET
Conceit, more rich in matter than in words,   30
Brags of his substance, not of ornament.   31
They are but beggars that can count their worth.
But my true love is grown to such excess
I cannot sum up sum of half my wealth.   34

FRIAR LAURENCE
Come, come with me, and we will make short work;
For, by your leaves, you shall not stay alone
Till Holy Church incorporate two in one.   *[Exeunt.]*

✤

13 confounds destroys   **18 gossamer** spider's thread   **19 wanton**
playful   **20 vanity** transitory human love   **21 ghostly** spiritual
22 thank thee i.e., give a kiss in thanks for your greeting   **23 As . . .
much** i.e., then I greet him with a kiss in repayment, lest I be overpaid
25 that if   **26 blazon** describe set forth. (A heraldic term.)   **28 Unfold**
make known.   **imagined** i.e., unexpressed   **29 in either** from each
other   **30–31 Conceit . . . ornament** true understanding, more enriched
by the actual reality (of love) than by mere words, finds more worth in
the substance of that reality than in outward show   **34 sum up sum**
add up the total

3.1   *Enter Mercutio, Benvolio, and men.*

BENVOLIO
  I pray thee, good Mercutio, let's retire.
  The day is hot, the Capels are abroad,   2
  And if we meet we shall not scape a brawl,
  For now, these hot days, is the mad blood stirring.

MERCUTIO Thou art like one of these fellows that when
he enters the confines of a tavern, claps me his sword
upon the table and says, "God send me no need of
thee!" and by the operation of the second cup draws 8
him on the drawer, when indeed there is no need.   9

BENVOLIO Am I like such a fellow?

MERCUTIO Come, come, thou art as hot a Jack in thy 11
mood as any in Italy, and as soon moved to be moody, 12
and as soon moody to be moved.   13

BENVOLIO And what to?

MERCUTIO Nay, an there were two such, we should 15
have none shortly, for one would kill the other. Thou!
Why, thou wilt quarrel with a man that hath a hair
more or a hair less in his beard than thou hast. Thou
wilt quarrel with a man for cracking nuts, having no
other reason but because thou hast hazel eyes. What
eye but such an eye would spy out such a quarrel? Thy
head is as full of quarrels as an egg is full of meat, and 22
yet thy head hath been beaten as addle as an egg for 23
quarreling. Thou hast quarreled with a man for cough-
ing in the street, because he hath wakened thy dog that
hath lain asleep in the sun. Didst thou not fall out with
a tailor for wearing his new doublet before Easter? 27
With another, for tying his new shoes with old rib-
bon? And yet thou wilt tutor me from quarreling!

BENVOLIO An I were so apt to quarrel as thou art, any
man should buy the fee simple of my life for an hour 31
and a quarter.   32

3.1. Location: Verona. A public place.
2 Capels Capulets **8–9 draws . . . drawer** draws his sword against the
tapster or waiter **9 there is no need** i.e., of his sword **11 as hot a Jack** as
hot-tempered a fellow **12 moody** angry **13 to be moved** at being pro-
voked **15 an** if **22 meat** i.e., edible matter **23 addle** addled, confused
27 doublet man's jacket **31 fee simple** outright possession **31–32 an hour
. . . quarter** i.e., my life would last no longer in such circumstances

MERCUTIO   The fee simple! O simple!   33

    Enter Tybalt, Petruchio, and others.

BENVOLIO   By my head, here comes the Capulets.

MERCUTIO   By my heel, I care not.

TYBALT [*To his companions*]
    Follow me close, for I will speak to them.—
    Gentlemen, good e'en. A word with one of you.

MERCUTIO   And but one word with one of us? Couple it
with something: make it a word and a blow.

TYBALT   You shall find me apt enough to that, sir, an
you will give me occasion.

MERCUTIO   Could you not take some occasion without
giving?

TYBALT   Mercutio, thou consortest with Romeo.   44

MERCUTIO   "Consort"? What, dost thou make us minstrels? An thou make minstrels of us, look to hear
nothing but discords. Here's my fiddlestick; here's   47
that shall make you dance. Zounds, "consort"!   48

BENVOLIO
    We talk here in the public haunt of men.
    Either withdraw unto some private place,
    Or reason coldly of your grievances,   51
    Or else depart; here all eyes gaze on us.   52

MERCUTIO
    Men's eyes were made to look, and let them gaze.
    I will not budge for no man's pleasure, I.

    Enter Romeo.

TYBALT
    Well, peace be with you, sir. Here comes my man.

MERCUTIO
    But I'll be hanged, sir, if he wear your livery.   56
    Marry, go before to field, he'll be your follower;   57
    Your worship in that sense may call him "man."   58

---

33 simple stupid   **44 consortest** keep company with. (But Mercutio
quibbles on its musical sense of "accompany" or "play together.")
47 fiddlestick (Mercutio means his sword.)   **48 that** that which.
Zounds i.e., by God's (Christ's) wounds   **51 coldly** calmly   **52 depart** go
away separately   **56 livery** servant's costume. (Mercutio deliberately
mistakes Tybalt's phrase *my man* to mean "my servant.")   **57 field** field
where a duel might occur   **58 Your worship** (A title of honor used here
with mock politeness.)

TYBALT
  Romeo, the love I bear thee can afford
  No better term than this: thou art a villain.

ROMEO
  Tybalt, the reason that I have to love thee
  Doth much excuse the appertaining rage   62
  To such a greeting. Villain am I none.
  Therefore, farewell. I see thou knowest me not.

TYBALT
  Boy, this shall not excuse the injuries
  That thou hast done me. Therefore turn and draw.

ROMEO
  I do protest I never injured thee,
  But love thee better than thou canst devise   68
  Till thou shalt know the reason of my love.
  And so, good Capulet—which name I tender   70
  As dearly as mine own—be satisfied.

MERCUTIO
  O calm, dishonorable, vile submission!
  Alla stoccata carries it away.   *[He draws.]* 73
  Tybalt, you ratcatcher, will you walk?   74

TYBALT   What wouldst thou have with me?

MERCUTIO   Good king of cats, nothing but one of your
  nine lives, that I mean to make bold withal, and, as 77
  you shall use me hereafter, dry-beat the rest of the 78
  eight. Will you pluck your sword out of his pilcher by 79
  the ears? Make haste, lest mine be about your ears ere
  it be out.

TYBALT   I am for you.   *[He draws.]*

ROMEO
  Gentle Mercutio, put thy rapier up.

MERCUTIO   Come, sir, your *passado*.   *[They fight.]* 84

ROMEO
  Draw, Benvolio, beat down their weapons.
  Gentlemen, for shame, forbear this outrage!

---

62 excuse . . . rage mollify the angry reaction appropriate   **68 devise**
understand   **70 tender** value   **73 Alla stoccata** at the thrust (Italian);
i.e., Tybalt, with his fine fencing phrases, *carries it away,* wins the day
74 ratcatcher (An allusion to Tybalt as king of cats; see 2.4.19.)
77 make bold withal make free with   **78 dry-beat** beat soundly (without
drawing blood)   **79 his pilcher** its scabbard   **84 passado** forward
thrust. (Said derisively.)

Tybalt, Mercutio, the Prince expressly hath
Forbid this bandying in Verona streets.
Hold, Tybalt! Good Mercutio!

> [*Tybalt under Romeo's arm stabs Mercutio.*]
>> *Away Tybalt* [*with his followers*].

MERCUTIO   I am hurt.   89
A plague o' both your houses! I am sped.   90
Is he gone, and hath nothing?
BENVOLIO   What, art thou hurt?
MERCUTIO
Ay, ay, a scratch, a scratch; marry, 'tis enough.
Where is my page? Go, villain, fetch a surgeon.

> [*Exit Page.*]

ROMEO
Courage, man, the hurt cannot be much.
MERCUTIO   No, 'tis not so deep as a well, nor so wide as
a church door, but 'tis enough, 'twill serve. Ask for me
tomorrow, and you shall find me a grave man. I am   97
peppered, I warrant, for this world. A plague o' both   98
your houses! Zounds, a dog, a rat, a mouse, a cat, to
scratch a man to death! A braggart, a rogue, a villain,
that fights by the book of arithmetic! Why the devil   101
came you between us? I was hurt under your arm.
ROMEO   I thought all for the best.
MERCUTIO
Help me into some house, Benvolio,
Or I shall faint. A plague o' both your houses!
They have made worm's meat of me. I have it,
And soundly too. Your houses!

> *Exit* [*supported by Benvolio*].

ROMEO
This gentleman, the Prince's near ally,   108
My very friend, hath got this mortal hurt   109
In my behalf; my reputation stained
With Tybalt's slander—Tybalt, that an hour
Hath been my cousin! O sweet Juliet,   112

---

89 s.d. Away Tybalt (Some editors assign this as a speech to Petruchio.)   **90 sped** done for   **97 grave** (Mercutio thus puns with his last
breath.)   **98 peppered** finished, done for   **101 by . . . arithmetic** by the
numbers, as in a textbook on fencing   **108 ally** kinsman   **109 very**
true   **112 cousin** kinsman

Thy beauty hath made me effeminate,   113
And in my temper softened valor's steel!   114

    Enter Benvolio.

BENVOLIO
O Romeo, Romeo, brave Mercutio is dead!
That gallant spirit hath aspired the clouds,   116
Which too untimely here did scorn the earth.

ROMEO
This day's black fate on more days doth depend;   118
This but begins the woe others must end.   119

    [*Enter Tybalt.*]   Foreshadowing

BENVOLIO
Here comes the furious Tybalt back again.

ROMEO
Alive in triumph, and Mercutio slain!
Away to heaven, respective lenity,   122
And fire-eyed fury be my conduct now!   123
Now, Tybalt, take the "villain" back again
That late thou gavest me, for Mercutio's soul
Is but a little way above our heads,
Staying for thine to keep him company.
Either thou or I, or both, must go with him.

TYBALT
Thou, wretched boy, that didst consort him here,
Shalt with him hence.

ROMEO   This shall determine that.

                     They fight. Tybalt falls.

BENVOLIO   Romeo, away, begone!
The citizens are up, and Tybalt slain.
Stand not amazed. The Prince will doom thee death   133
If thou art taken. Hence, begone, away!

ROMEO
O, I am fortune's fool!

BENVOLIO   Why dost thou stay?   135

                     Exit Romeo.

---

113 effeminate weak **114 temper** disposition (but with a play on the
tempering of a steel sword) **116 aspired** ascended to **118 depend** hang
over threateningly **119 others** other days to come **122 respective
lenity** considerate gentleness **123 conduct** guide **133 amazed** dazed.
doom thee death sentence you to death **135 fool** dupe

Enter Citizens.

FIRST CITIZEN
Which way ran he that killed Mercutio?
Tybalt, that murderer, which way ran he?
BENVOLIO
There lies that Tybalt.
FIRST CITIZEN   Up, sir, go with me.
I charge thee in the Prince's name, obey.

*Enter Prince [attended], old Montague, Capulet,
their Wives, and all.*

PRINCE
Where are the vile beginners of this fray?
BENVOLIO
O noble Prince, I can discover all   141
The unlucky manage of this fatal brawl.   142
There lies the man, slain by young Romeo,
That slew thy kinsman, brave Mercutio.
CAPULET'S WIFE
Tybalt, my cousin! O my brother's child!
O Prince! O cousin! Husband! O, the blood is spilled
Of my dear kinsman! Prince, as thou art true,
For blood of ours shed blood of Montague.
O cousin, cousin!
PRINCE
Benvolio, who began this bloody fray?
BENVOLIO
Tybalt, here slain, whom Romeo's hand did slay.
Romeo, that spoke him fair, bid him bethink   152
How nice the quarrel was, and urged withal   153
Your high displeasure. All this—utterèd
With gentle breath, calm look, knees humbly bowed—
Could not take truce with the unruly spleen   156
Of Tybalt deaf to peace, but that he tilts
With piercing steel at bold Mercutio's breast,
Who, all as hot, turns deadly point to point,
And, with a martial scorn, with one hand beats
Cold death aside and with the other sends
It back to Tybalt, whose dexterity

141 discover reveal **142 manage** conduct **152 fair** civilly. **bethink**
consider **153 nice** trivial. **withal** besides **156 take truce** make peace

Retorts it. Romeo he cries aloud,   163
"Hold, friends! Friends, part!" and swifter than his
  tongue
His agile arm beats down their fatal points,
And twixt them rushes; underneath whose arm
An envious thrust from Tybalt hit the life   167
Of stout Mercutio, and then Tybalt fled;   168
But by and by comes back to Romeo,
Who had but newly entertained revenge,   170
And to 't they go like lightning, for, ere I
Could draw to part them was stout Tybalt slain,
And, as he fell, did Romeo turn and fly.
This is the truth, or let Benvolio die.

CAPULET'S WIFE
He is a kinsman to the Montague.
Affection makes him false; he speaks not true.   176
Some twenty of them fought in this black strife,
And all those twenty could but kill one life.
I beg for justice, which thou, Prince, must give.
Romeo slew Tybalt; Romeo must not live.

PRINCE
Romeo slew him, he slew Mercutio.
Who now the price of his dear blood doth owe?

MONTAGUE
Not Romeo, Prince, he was Mercutio's friend;
His fault concludes but what the law should end,   184
The life of Tybalt.

PRINCE   And for that offense
Immediately we do exile him hence.
I have an interest in your heart's proceeding;
My blood for your rude brawls doth lie a-bleeding;   188
But I'll amerce you with so strong a fine   189
That you shall all repent the loss of mine.
I will be deaf to pleading and excuses;
Nor tears nor prayers shall purchase out abuses.   192
Therefore use none. Let Romeo hence in haste,   193
Else, when he is found, that hour is his last.   194

---

163 Retorts returns   **167 envious** malicious   **168 stout** brave   **170 entertained** harbored thoughts of   **176 Affection** partiality   **184 concludes but** only finishes   **188 My blood** i.e., blood of my kinsman   **189 amerce** punish by a fine   **192 Nor tears** neither tears.   **purchase out abuses** redeem misdeeds   **193 hence** depart   **194 Else** otherwise

Bear hence this body and attend our will.   195
Mercy but murders, pardoning those that kill.
                    Exeunt, [*some carrying Tybalt's body*].

❖

3.2   *Enter Juliet alone.*

JULIET
                    ~Soliloquy~
Gallop apace, you fiery-footed steeds,   1
Towards Phoebus' lodging! Such a wagoner   2
As Phaëthon would whip you to the west   3
And bring in cloudy night immediately.
Spread thy close curtain, love-performing night,   5
That runaways' eyes may wink, and Romeo   6
Leap to these arms, untalked of and unseen.
Lovers can see to do their amorous rites
By their own beauties; or, if love be blind,
It best agrees with night. Come, civil night,   10
Thou sober-suited matron all in black,
And learn me how to lose a winning match   12
Played for a pair of stainless maidenhoods.
Hood my unmanned blood, bating in my cheeks,   14
With thy black mantle till strange love grow bold,   15
Think true love acted simple modesty.   16
Come, night. Come, Romeo. Come, thou day in night;
For thou wilt lie upon the wings of night
Whiter than new snow upon a raven's back.
Come, gentle night, come, loving, black-browed night,

---

195 attend our will be on hand to hear further judgment

3.2. Location: Verona. Capulet's house.
1 apace quickly.   **steeds** i.e., the horses of the sun god's chariot
2 Phoebus (Often equated with Helios, the sun god.)   **lodging** i.e., in the
west, below the horizon   **2–3 Such . . . Phaëthon** i.e., a rash charioteer
like Phaëthon, who would quickly bring the day to an end. (Phaëthon
was son of the sun god, and was allowed to assume the reins of the sun
for a day; not being able to restrain the steeds, he had to be slain by the
thunderbolt of Zeus.)   **5 close** enclosing   **6 runaways'** (Refers to the
horses of the sun chariot that ran away with Phaëthon?)   **wink** shut,
close   **10 civil** circumspect, somberly attired   **12 learn** teach   **14 Hood**
cover. (A term in falconry; the hawk's eyes were covered so that it would
not *bate* or beat its wings.)   **unmanned** untamed (in falconry; with a
pun on "unmarried")   **15 strange** diffident   **16 Think** i.e., and think

tragically ironic

Give me my Romeo, and when I shall die   21
Take him and cut him out in little stars,
And he will make the face of heaven so fine
That all the world will be in love with night
And pay no worship to the garish sun.   25
O, I have bought the mansion of a love   26
But not possessed it, and though I am sold,
Not yet enjoyed. So tedious is this day
As is the night before some festival
To an impatient child that hath new robes
And may not wear them. O, here comes my nurse,   31

    Enter Nurse, with cords.

And she brings news, and every tongue that speaks
But Romeo's name speaks heavenly eloquence.
Now, Nurse, what news? What hast thou there? The
    cords
That Romeo bid thee fetch?
NURSE   Ay, ay, the cords.
    [*She throws them down.*]
JULIET
Ay me, what news? Why dost thou wring thy hands?
NURSE
Ah, weraday! He's dead, he's dead, he's dead!   37
We are undone, lady, we are undone!
Alack the day, he's gone, he's killed, he's dead!
JULIET
Can heaven be so envious?
NURSE   Romeo can,   40
Though heaven cannot. O Romeo, Romeo!
Whoever would have thought it? Romeo!
JULIET
What devil art thou, that dost torment me thus?
This torture should be roared in dismal hell.
Hath Romeo slain himself? Say thou but "Ay,"
And that bare vowel "I" shall poison more   46

21 I (Often emended to *he*, following Quarto 4, but Juliet may mean that
when she is dead she will share Romeo's beauty with the world. Dying
may also hint at sexual climax.)   **25 garish** dazzling   **26 mansion** dwelling   **31 s.d. cords** ropes (for the ladder)   **37 weraday** i.e., wellaway,
alas   **40 envious** malicious   **46 "I"** (Pronounced identically with *ay*.)

Than the death-darting eye of cockatrice.   47
I am not I, if there be such an "Ay,"
Or those eyes shut, that makes thee answer "Ay."   49
If he be slain, say "Ay," or if not, "No."
Brief sounds determine of my weal or woe.   51

NURSE
I saw the wound. I saw it with mine eyes—
God save the mark!—here on his manly breast.   53
A piteous corpse, a bloody piteous corpse;
Pale, pale as ashes, all bedaubed in blood,
All in gore-blood. I swoonèd at the sight.   56

JULIET
O, break, my heart! Poor bankrupt, break at once!
To prison, eyes; ne'er look on liberty!
Vile earth, to earth resign; end motion here,   59
And thou and Romeo press one heavy bier!   60

NURSE
O Tybalt, Tybalt, the best friend I had!
O courteous Tybalt! Honest gentleman!
That ever I should live to see thee dead!

JULIET
What storm is this that blows so contrary?
Is Romeo slaughtered, and is Tybalt dead?
My dearest cousin, and my dearer lord?
Then, dreadful trumpet, sound the general doom!   67
For who is living, if those two are gone?

NURSE
Tybalt is gone, and Romeo banishèd;
Romeo that killed him, he is banishèd.

JULIET
O God! Did Romeo's hand shed Tybalt's blood?

NURSE
It did, it did. Alas the day it did!

JULIET
O serpent heart, hid with a flowering face!   73

---

47 cockatrice i.e., basilisk, a mythical serpent that could kill by its
look   **49 those eyes shut** i.e., if Romeo's eyes are shut (in death)
51 weal welfare, happiness   **53 God save the mark** (A familiar oath
originally intended to avert ill omen.)   **56 gore-blood** clotted blood
59 Vile earth i.e., my body.   **resign** surrender, return   **60 press** weigh
down.   **bier** litter for carrying corpses   **67 trumpet** i.e., the last trumpet.   **general doom** Day of Judgment   **73 hid with** hidden by.   **flowering** i.e., fair, like that of the serpent in the Garden of Eden

Did ever dragon keep so fair a cave? *oxymorons* 74
Beautiful tyrant! Fiend angelical!
Dove-feathered raven! Wolvish-ravening lamb!
Despisèd substance of divinest show! 77
Just opposite to what thou justly seem'st, 78
A damnèd saint, an honorable villain!
O nature, what hadst thou to do in hell *speaking*
When thou didst bower the spirit of a fiend *against* 81
In mortal paradise of such sweet flesh? *Romeo*
Was ever book containing such vile matter
So fairly bound? O, that deceit should dwell
In such a gorgeous palace!

NURSE　　　　　　　　　　There's no trust,
No faith, no honesty in men; all perjured,
All forsworn, all naught, all dissemblers. 87
Ah, where's my man? Give me some aqua vitae. 88
These griefs, these woes, these sorrows make me old.
Shame come to Romeo!

JULIET　　　　　　　　　Blistered be thy tongue
For such a wish! He was not born to shame.
Upon his brow shame is ashamed to sit;
For 'tis a throne where honor may be crowned
Sole monarch of the universal earth.
O, what a beast was I to chide at him!

NURSE
Will you speak well of him that killed your cousin?

JULIET
Shall I speak ill of him that is my husband?
Ah, poor my lord, what tongue shall smooth thy name 98
When I, thy three-hours wife, have mangled it?
But wherefore, villain, didst thou kill my cousin?
That villain cousin would have killed my husband.
Back, foolish tears, back to your native spring!
Your tributary drops belong to woe, 103
Which you, mistaking, offer up to joy.

---

74 keep occupy, guard.　**cave** i.e., one with treasure in it　**77 show**
appearance　**78 Just** precisely (with a play on *justly*, truly)　**81 bower**
give lodging to　**87 naught** worthless, evil　**88 aqua vitae** alcoholic
spirits　**98 poor my lord** my poor lord.　**smooth** speak kindly of
103 Your . . . woe i.e., you should be shed, offered as a tribute, on some
occasion of real woe

My husband lives, that Tybalt would have slain,   105
And Tybalt's dead, that would have slain my husband.
All this is comfort. Wherefore weep I then?
Some word there was, worser than Tybalt's death,
That murdered me. I would forget it fain,   109
But O, it presses to my memory
Like damnèd guilty deeds to sinners' minds:
"Tybalt is dead, and Romeo—banishèd."
That "banishèd," that one word "banishèd,"
Hath slain ten thousand Tybalts. Tybalt's death
Was woe enough, if it had ended there;
Or, if sour woe delights in fellowship
And needly will be ranked with other griefs,   117
Why followed not, when she said "Tybalt's dead,"
"Thy father," or "thy mother," nay, or both,
Which modern lamentation might have moved?   120
But with a rearward following Tybalt's death,   121
"Romeo is banishèd"—to speak that word
Is father, mother, Tybalt, Romeo, Juliet,
All slain, all dead. "Romeo is banishèd!"
There is no end, no limit, measure, bound,
In that word's death; no words can that woe sound.   126
Where is my father and my mother, Nurse?

NURSE
Weeping and wailing over Tybalt's corpse.
Will you go to them? I will bring you thither.

JULIET
Wash they his wounds with tears? Mine shall be spent,
When theirs are dry, for Romeo's banishment.
Take up those cords. Poor ropes, you are beguiled,
Both you and I, for Romeo is exiled.
He made you for a highway to my bed;
But I, a maid, die maiden-widowèd.
Come, cords, come, Nurse. I'll to my wedding bed,
And death, not Romeo, take my maidenhead!

NURSE [Taking up the cords]
Hie to your chamber. I'll find Romeo
To comfort you. I wot well where he is.   139

105 that whom   **109 fain** gladly   **117 needly** of necessity.   **ranked with**
accompanied by   **120 modern** ordinary   **121 rearward** rearguard
126 sound (1) fathom (2) express   **139 wot** know

Hark ye, your Romeo will be here at night.
I'll to him. He is hid at Laurence' cell.

FRIAR LAURENCE

JULIET

O, find him! Give this ring to my true knight,
                              [*Giving a ring*]
And bid him come to take his last farewell.
                              Exeunt [*separately*].

❖

3.3 *Enter Friar* [*Laurence*].

FRIAR LAURENCE

Romeo, come forth; come forth, thou fearful man. 1
Affliction is enamored of thy parts, 2
And thou art wedded to calamity.

  [*Enter*] *Romeo.*

ROMEO

Father, what news? What is the Prince's doom? 4
What sorrow craves acquaintance at my hand
That I yet know not?

FRIAR LAURENCE   Too familiar

Is my dear son with such sour company.
I bring thee tidings of the Prince's doom.

ROMEO

What less than doomsday is the Prince's doom? 9

FRIAR LAURENCE

A gentler judgment vanished from his lips: 10
Not body's death, but body's banishment.

ROMEO

Ha, banishment? Be merciful, say "death";
For exile hath more terror in his look,
Much more than death. Do not say "banishment."

FRIAR LAURENCE

Here from Verona art thou banishèd.
Be patient, for the world is broad and wide.

3.3. Location: Verona. Friar Laurence's cell.
1 fearful full of fear (but also inspiring fear as a tragic figure) **2 parts**
qualities **4 doom** judgment **9 doomsday** the Day of Judgment, i.e.,
death **10 vanished** issued (into air)

ROMEO
  There is no world without Verona walls   17
  But purgatory, torture, hell itself.
  Hence "banishèd" is banished from the world,
  And world's exile is death. Then "banishèd"   20
  Is death mistermed. Calling death "banishèd,"
  Thou cutt'st my head off with a golden ax
  And smilest upon the stroke that murders me.

FRIAR LAURENCE
  O deadly sin! O rude unthankfulness!
  Thy fault our law calls death, but the kind Prince,   25
  Taking thy part, hath rushed aside the law   26
  And turned that black word "death" to "banishment."
  This is dear mercy, and thou seest it not.

ROMEO
  'Tis torture, and not mercy. Heaven is here
  Where Juliet lives, and every cat and dog
  And little mouse, every unworthy thing,
  Live here in heaven and may look on her,
  But Romeo may not. More validity,   33
  More honorable state, more courtship lives   34
  In carrion flies than Romeo. They may seize
  On the white wonder of dear Juliet's hand
  And steal immortal blessing from her lips,
  Who even in pure and vestal modesty   38
  Still blush, as thinking their own kisses sin;   39
  But Romeo may not, he is banishèd.
  Flies may do this, but I from this must fly.
  They are free men, but I am banishèd.
  And sayest thou yet that exile is not death?
  Hadst thou no poison mixed, no sharp-ground knife,
  No sudden mean of death, though ne'er so mean,   45
  But "banishèd" to kill me? "Banishèd"?
  O Friar, the damnèd use that word in hell;
  Howling attends it. How hast thou the heart,
  Being a divine, a ghostly confessor,

---

17 without outside of   **20 world's exile** exile from the world   **25 Thy fault . . . death** for your crime the law demands a death sentence
26 rushed thrust (aside)   **33 validity** value   **34 courtship** (1) courtliness (2) occasion for wooing   **38 vestal** maidenly   **39 their own kisses** i.e., their touching one another   **45 mean . . . mean** means . . . base

A sin absolver, and my friend professed,
To mangle me with that word "banishèd"?

FRIAR LAURENCE
Thou fond mad man, hear me a little speak.   52

ROMEO
O, thou wilt speak again of banishment.

FRIAR LAURENCE
I'll give thee armor to keep off that word,
Adversity's sweet milk, philosophy,
To comfort thee, though thou art banishèd.

ROMEO
Yet "banishèd"? Hang up philosophy!   57
Unless philosophy can make a Juliet,
Displant a town, reverse a prince's doom,   59
It helps not, it prevails not. Talk no more.

FRIAR LAURENCE
O, then I see that madmen have no ears.

ROMEO
How should they, when that wise men have no eyes?

FRIAR LAURENCE
Let me dispute with thee of thy estate.   63

ROMEO
Thou canst not speak of that thou dost not feel.   64
Wert thou as young as I, Juliet thy love,
An hour but married, Tybalt murderèd,
Doting like me and like me banishèd,
Then mightst thou speak, then mightst thou tear thy
     hair,
And fall upon the ground, as I do now,
Taking the measure of an unmade grave.
                                        [*He falls upon the ground.*]
                                        Knock [*within*].

FRIAR LAURENCE
Arise. One knocks. Good Romeo, hide thyself.

ROMEO
Not I, unless the breath of heartsick groans,
Mistlike, infold me from the search of eyes.   *Knock.*

FRIAR LAURENCE
Hark, how they knock!—Who's there?—Romeo, arise.

---

52 fond foolish   **57 Yet** still   **59 Displant** uproot   **63 dispute** reason.
estate situation   **64 that** that which

Thou wilt be taken.—Stay awhile!—Stand up.

Knock.

Run to my study.—By and by!—God's will,
What simpleness is this?—I come, I come!   *Knock.* 77
Who knocks so hard? Whence come you? What's your
will?   [*Going to the door.*]

NURSE [*Within*]
Let me come in, and you shall know my errand.
I come from Lady Juliet.

FRIAR LAURENCE   Welcome, then.

[*He opens the door.*]

    Enter Nurse.

NURSE
O holy Friar, O, tell me, holy Friar,
Where's my lady's lord, where's Romeo?

FRIAR LAURENCE
There on the ground, with his own tears made drunk.

NURSE
O, he is even in my mistress' case,   84
Just in her case! O woeful sympathy!   85
Piteous predicament! Even so lies she,
Blubbering and weeping, weeping and blubbering.—
Stand up, stand up! Stand, an you be a man.   88
For Juliet's sake, for her sake, rise and stand!
Why should you fall into so deep an O?   90

ROMEO   Nurse!   [*He rises.*]

NURSE
Ah, sir, ah, sir! Death's the end of all.

ROMEO
Spakest thou of Juliet? How is it with her?
Doth not she think me an old murderer,   94
Now I have stained the childhood of our joy
With blood removed but little from her own?
Where is she? And how doth she? And what says
My concealed lady to our canceled love?   98

---

77 simpleness foolishness   **84 even** exactly.   **case** situation   **85 woeful
sympathy** mutuality of grief   **88 an** if   **90 an O** a fit of groaning
94 old hardened   **98 concealed** secret.   **canceled** nullified (by the
impending exile)

NURSE
  O, she says nothing, sir, but weeps and weeps,
  And now falls on her bed, and then starts up,
  And "Tybalt" calls, and then on Romeo cries,   101
  And then down falls again.
ROMEO   As if that name,
  Shot from the deadly level of a gun,   103
  Did murder her, as that name's cursèd hand
  Murdered her kinsman. O, tell me, Friar, tell me,
  In what vile part of this anatomy
  Doth my name lodge? Tell me, that I may sack   107
  The hateful mansion.
          [*He draws a weapon, but is restrained.*]
FRIAR LAURENCE   Hold thy desperate hand!
  Art thou a man? Thy form cries out thou art;
  Thy tears are womanish, thy wild acts denote
  The unreasonable fury of a beast.
  Unseemly woman in a seeming man,
  And ill-beseeming beast in seeming both!
  Thou hast amazed me. By my holy order,
  I thought thy disposition better tempered.   115
  Hast thou slain Tybalt? Wilt thou slay thyself,
  And slay thy lady, that in thy life lives,
  By doing damnèd hate upon thyself?
  Why railest thou on thy birth, the heaven, and earth,
  Since birth, and heaven, and earth, all three do meet 120
  In thee at once, which thou at once wouldst lose?
  Fie, fie, thou shamest thy shape, thy love, thy wit,   122
  Which, like a usurer, abound'st in all,   123
  And usest none in that true use indeed   124
  Which should bedeck thy shape, thy love, thy wit.
  Thy noble shape is but a form of wax,   126
  Digressing from the valor of a man;   127
  Thy dear love sworn but hollow perjury,
  Killing that love which thou hast vowed to cherish;   129

---

101 on Romeo cries exclaims against Romeo, calls his name   **103 level**
aim   **107 sack** destroy   **115 tempered** harmonized, balanced
120 heaven, and earth i.e., soul and body   **122 wit** intellect   **123 Which**
(you) who.   **all** all capabilities   **124 true use** i.e., proper use of your
resources, not usury   **126 form of wax** waxwork, mere outer form
127 Digressing if it deviates   **129 Killing** if it kills

Thy wit, that ornament to shape and love,
Misshapen in the conduct of them both,   131
Like powder in a skilless soldier's flask   132
Is set afire by thine own ignorance,
And thou dismembered with thine own defense.   134
What, rouse thee, man! Thy Juliet is alive,
For whose dear sake thou wast but lately dead;   136
There art thou happy. Tybalt would kill thee,   137
But thou slewest Tybalt; there art thou happy.
The law that threatened death becomes thy friend
And turns it to exile; there art thou happy.
A pack of blessings light upon thy back,
Happiness courts thee in her best array,
But like a mishavèd and sullen wench   143
Thou pouts upon thy fortune and thy love.
Take heed, take heed, for such die miserable.
Go, get thee to thy love, as was decreed;
Ascend her chamber; hence and comfort her.
But look thou stay not till the watch be set,   148
For then thou canst not pass to Mantua,
Where thou shalt live till we can find a time
To blaze your marriage, reconcile your friends,   151
Beg pardon of the Prince, and call thee back
With twenty hundred thousand times more joy
Than thou went'st forth in lamentation.
Go before, Nurse. Commend me to thy lady,
And bid her hasten all the house to bed,
Which heavy sorrow makes them apt unto.
Romeo is coming.

NURSE
O Lord, I could have stayed here all the night
To hear good counsel. O, what learning is!—
My lord, I'll tell my lady you will come.

ROMEO
Do so, and bid my sweet prepare to chide.

---

131 **conduct** guidance   132 **powder** gunpowder.   **flask** powder horn
134 **dismembered with** blown to pieces by.   **thine own defense** that which
should defend you, i.e., your *wit* or intellect   136 **wast . . . dead** i.e.,
only recently were wishing yourself dead (see l. 70)   137 **happy** fortunate
143 **mishavèd** misbehaved   148 **the watch be set** guards be posted (at the
city gates)   151 **blaze** publish, divulge.   **friends** relations

NURSE [*Giving a ring*]
  Here, sir, a ring she bid me give you, sir.
  Hie you, make haste, for it grows very late.   [*Exit.*]

ROMEO
  How well my comfort is revived by this!   165

FRIAR LAURENCE
  Go hence. Good night. And here stands all your state: 166
  Either be gone before the watch be set,
  Or by the break of day disguised from hence.
  Sojourn in Mantua. I'll find out your man,
  And he shall signify from time to time
  Every good hap to you that chances here.   171
  Give me thy hand. 'Tis late. Farewell, good night.

ROMEO
  But that a joy past joy calls out on me,
  It were a grief so brief to part with thee.   174
  Farewell.   *Exeunt* [*separately*].

✚

3.4   *Enter old Capulet, his Wife, and Paris.*

CAPULET
  Things have fallen out, sir, so unluckily   1
  That we have had no time to move our daughter.   2
  Look you, she loved her kinsman Tybalt dearly,
  And so did I. Well, we were born to die.
  'Tis very late. She'll not come down tonight.
  I promise you, but for your company   6
  I would have been abed an hour ago.

PARIS
  These times of woe afford no times to woo.
  Madam, good night. Commend me to your daughter.

WIFE
  I will, and know her mind early tomorrow.
  Tonight she's mewed up to her heaviness.   11

---

165 comfort happiness   **166 here . . . state** your fortune depends on
what follows   **171 good hap** fortunate event   **174 brief** quickly

3.4. Location: Verona. Capulet's house.
1 fallen out happened   **2 move** persuade   **6 promise** assure   **11 mewed
up to** cooped up with. (A falconry term.)   **heaviness** sorrow

CAPULET
  Sir Paris, I will make a desperate tender   12
  Of my child's love. I think she will be ruled
  In all respects by me; nay, more, I doubt it not.
  Wife, go you to her ere you go to bed.
  Acquaint her here of my son Paris' love,
  And bid her, mark you me, on Wednesday next—   17
  But soft, what day is this?
PARIS   Monday, my lord.
CAPULET
  Monday! Ha, ha! Well, Wednesday is too soon;
  O' Thursday let it be. O' Thursday, tell her,
  She shall be married to this noble earl.
  Will you be ready? Do you like this haste?
  We'll keep no great ado—a friend or two;
  For hark you, Tybalt being slain so late,   24
  It may be thought we held him carelessly,   25
  Being our kinsman, if we revel much.
  Therefore we'll have some half a dozen friends,
  And there an end. But what say you to Thursday?
PARIS
  My lord, I would that Thursday were tomorrow.
CAPULET
  Well, get you gone. O' Thursday be it, then.
  [*To his Wife.*] Go you to Juliet ere you go to bed;
  Prepare her, wife, against this wedding day.—   32
  Farewell, my lord.—Light to my chamber, ho!—
  Afore me, it is so very late   34
  That we may call it early by and by.
  Good night.   *Exeunt.*

❧

---

12 desperate tender bold offer   **17 mark you me** are you paying attention   **24 late** recently   **25 held him carelessly** did not regard him
highly   **32 against** in anticipation of   **34 Afore me** i.e., by my life.
(A mild oath.)

3.5   *Enter Romeo and Juliet aloft [at the window].*

JULIET
   Wilt thou be gone? It is not yet near day.
   It was the nightingale, and not the lark,
   That pierced the fearful hollow of thine ear;   3
   Nightly she sings on yond pomegranate tree.
   Believe me, love, it was the nightingale.

ROMEO
   It was the lark, the herald of the morn,
   No nightingale. Look, love, what envious streaks
   Do lace the severing clouds in yonder east.   8
   Night's candles are burnt out, and jocund day   9
   Stands tiptoe on the misty mountain tops.
   I must be gone and live, or stay and die.

JULIET
   Yond light is not daylight, I know it, I.
   It is some meteor that the sun exhaled   13
   To be to thee this night a torchbearer
   And light thee on thy way to Mantua.
   Therefore stay yet. Thou need'st not to be gone.

ROMEO
   Let me be ta'en; let me be put to death.
   I am content, so thou wilt have it so.   18
   I'll say yon gray is not the morning's eye;
   'Tis but the pale reflex of Cynthia's brow.   20
   Nor that is not the lark whose notes do beat
   The vaulty heaven so high above our heads.
   I have more care to stay than will to go.   23
   Come, death, and welcome! Juliet wills it so.
   How is 't, my soul? Let's talk. It is not day.

JULIET
   It is, it is. Hie hence, begone, away!   26

3.5. Location: Verona. Capulet's orchard with Juliet's chamber window above, and subsequently (l. 68) the interior of Juliet's chamber.

3 fearful apprehensive, anxious   **8 severing** separating   **9 jocund** cheerful   **13 exhaled** i.e., has drawn out of the ground. (Meteors were thought to be vapors of luminous gas drawn up by the sun.)   **18 so thou** if you   **20 reflex** reflection.   **Cynthia's** the moon's   **23 care** desire, concern   **26 Hie hence** hasten away

It is the lark that sings so out of tune,
Straining harsh discords and unpleasing sharps.   28
Some say the lark makes sweet division;   29
This doth not so, for she divideth us.
Some say the lark and loathèd toad changed eyes;   31
O, now I would they had changed voices too,
Since arm from arm that voice doth us affray,   33
Hunting thee hence with hunt's-up to the day.   34
O, now begone! More light and light it grows.

ROMEO
More light and light, more dark and dark our woes!

Enter Nurse [hastily].

NURSE   Madam!
JULIET   Nurse?
NURSE
Your lady mother is coming to your chamber.
The day is broke; be wary, look about.   [*Exit.*]
JULIET
Then window, let day in, and let life out.
ROMEO
Farewell, farewell! One kiss, and I'll descend.
          [*They kiss. He climbs down from the window.*]
JULIET
Art thou gone so? Love, lord, ay, husband, friend!   43
I must hear from thee every day in the hour,
For in a minute there are many days.
O, by this count I shall be much in years   46
Ere I again behold my Romeo!
ROMEO [*From below her window*]   Farewell!
I will omit no opportunity
That may convey my greetings, love, to thee.
JULIET
O, think'st thou we shall ever meet again?

---

28 sharps notes relatively high in pitch and hence discordant
29 division variations on a melody, made by dividing each note into
notes of briefer duration   **31 changed** exchanged. (A popular saying, to
account for the observation that the lark has very ordinary eyes and the
toad remarkable ones.)   **33 arm from arm** from one another's arms.
affray frighten   **34 hunt's-up** a song or tune to awaken huntsmen and,
later, a newly married couple   **43 friend** lover   **46 count** method of
calculation.   **much in years** very old

ROMEO

I doubt it not, and all these woes shall serve
For sweet discourses in our times to come.

JULIET

O God, I have an ill-divining soul!   54
Methinks I see thee, now thou art so low,
As one dead in the bottom of a tomb.
Either my eyesight fails or thou lookest pale.

Foreshadowing

ROMEO

And trust me, love, in my eye so do you.
Dry sorrow drinks our blood. Adieu, adieu!   *Exit.* 59

JULIET

O Fortune, Fortune! All men call thee fickle.
If thou art fickle, what dost thou with him
That is renowned for faith? Be fickle, Fortune.
For then, I hope, thou wilt not keep him long,
But send him back.

          Enter Mother [Capulet's Wife].

WIFE   Ho, daughter, are you up?

JULIET

Who is 't that calls? It is my lady mother.
Is she not down so late, or up so early?   66
What unaccustomed cause procures her hither?   67
                    [*She goeth down from the window.*]

WIFE

Why, how now, Juliet?

JULIET   Madam, I am not well.

WIFE

Evermore weeping for your cousin's death?
What, wilt thou wash him from his grave with tears?

---

54 ill-divining prophesying of evil   **59 Dry sorrow** (The heat of the body
in sorrow and despair was thought to descend into the bowels and dry
up the blood.)   **66 down** in bed   **67 procures** induces to come. (As indicated by the bracketed stage direction, which is from the first quarto,
Juliet, who has appeared until now at her "window" above the stage,
evidently descends quickly to the main stage and joins her mother for
the remainder of the scene. The stage, which before was to have been
imagined as Capulet's orchard, is now Juliet's chamber. Juliet's mother
has entered onto the main stage four lines earlier.)

An if thou couldst, thou couldst not make him live;   71
Therefore, have done. Some grief shows much of love,
But much of grief shows still some want of wit.   73

JULIET
Yet let me weep for such a feeling loss.   74

WIFE
So shall you feel the loss, but not the friend
Which you weep for.

JULIET   Feeling so the loss,
I cannot choose but ever weep the friend.

WIFE
Well, girl, thou weep'st not so much for his death
As that the villain lives which slaughtered him.

JULIET
What villain, madam?

WIFE   That same villain, Romeo.

JULIET [*Aside*]
Villain and he be many miles asunder.—
God pardon him! I do, with all my heart;
And yet no man like he doth grieve my heart.   83

WIFE
That is because the traitor murderer lives.

JULIET
Ay, madam, from the reach of these my hands.
Would none but I might venge my cousin's death!

WIFE
We will have vengeance for it, fear thou not.
Then weep no more. I'll send to one in Mantua,
Where that same banished runagate doth live,   89
Shall give him such an unaccustomed dram   90
That he shall soon keep Tybalt company.
And then, I hope, thou wilt be satisfied.

JULIET
Indeed, I never shall be satisfied
With Romeo till I behold him—dead—
Is my poor heart so for a kinsman vexed.

---

71 An if if   **73 wit** intellect   **74 feeling** deeply felt   **83 no man like he**
no man so much as he.   **grieve** (1) anger (2) grieve with longing. (Juliet
speaks to her mother throughout in intentional ambiguities, at ll. 86, 99,
100–102, etc.)   **89 runagate** renegade, fugitive   **90 Shall** who shall.
dram dose. (Literally, one-eighth of a fluid ounce.)

Madam, if you could find out but a man
To bear a poison, I would temper it,   97
That Romeo should, upon receipt thereof,
Soon sleep in quiet. O, how my heart abhors
To hear him named, and cannot come to him
To wreak the love I bore my cousin   101
Upon his body that hath slaughtered him!   102

WIFE
Find thou the means, and I'll find such a man.
But now I'll tell thee joyful tidings, girl.

JULIET
And joy comes well in such a needy time.
What are they, beseech your ladyship?

WIFE
Well, well, thou hast a careful father, child,   107
One who, to put thee from thy heaviness,   108
Hath sorted out a sudden day of joy   109
That thou expects not, nor I looked not for.

JULIET
Madam, in happy time, what day is that?

WIFE
Marry, my child, early next Thursday morn,   112
The gallant, young, and noble gentleman,
The County Paris, at Saint Peter's Church
Shall happily make thee there a joyful bride.

JULIET
Now, by Saint Peter's Church, and Peter too,
He shall not make me there a joyful bride!
I wonder at this haste, that I must wed
Ere he that should be husband comes to woo.
I pray you, tell my lord and father, madam,
I will not marry yet, and when I do I swear
It shall be Romeo, whom you know I hate,
Rather than Paris. These are news indeed!

WIFE
Here comes your father. Tell him so yourself,
And see how he will take it at your hands.

---

97 temper (1) mix, concoct (2) alloy, dilute   **101 wreak** (1) avenge
(2) bestow   **102 his body that** the body of him who   **107 careful** full of
care (for you)   **108 heaviness** sorrow   **109 sorted** chosen   **112 Marry**
i.e., by the Virgin Mary

Enter Capulet and Nurse.

CAPULET
When the sun sets, the earth doth drizzle dew,
But for the sunset of my brother's son
It rains downright.
How now, a conduit, girl? What, still in tears?   129
Evermore showering? In one little body
Thou counterfeits a bark, a sea, a wind;   131
For still thy eyes, which I may call the sea,
Do ebb and flow with tears; the bark thy body is,
Sailing in this salt flood; the winds, thy sighs,
Who, raging with thy tears, and they with them,
Without a sudden calm, will overset   136
Thy tempest-tossèd body.—How now, wife?
Have you delivered to her our decree?

WIFE
Ay, sir, but she will none, she gives you thanks.   139
I would the fool were married to her grave!

CAPULET
Soft, take me with you, take me with you, wife.   141
How? Will she none? Doth she not give us thanks?
Is she not proud? Doth she not count her blest,   143
Unworthy as she is, that we have wrought   144
So worthy a gentleman to be her bride?   145

JULIET
Not proud you have, but thankful that you have.
Proud can I never be of what I hate,
But thankful even for hate that is meant love.   148

CAPULET
How, how, how, how, chopped logic? What is this?   149
"Proud," and "I thank you," and "I thank you not,"
And yet "not proud"? Mistress minion, you,   151
Thank me no thankings, nor proud me no prouds,

---

129 conduit water pipe, fountain   **131 bark** sailing vessel   **136 Without
. . . calm** unless they quickly calm themselves   **139 will . . . thanks** says
"no thank you," she'll have none, no part of it   **141 take . . . you** let me
understand you   **143 count her** consider herself   **144 wrought** pro-
cured   **145 bride** bridegroom   **148 hate . . . love** i.e., that which is
hateful but which was meant lovingly   **149 chopped logic** a shallow and
sophistical argument, or arguer   **151 minion** spoiled darling, minx.

But fettle your fine joints 'gainst Thursday next   153
To go with Paris to Saint Peter's Church,
Or I will drag thee on a hurdle thither.   155
Out, you greensickness carrion! Out, you baggage!   156
You tallow-face!

WIFE [*To Capulet*] Fie, fie! What, are you mad?   157
JULIET [*Kneeling*]
 Good father, I beseech you on my knees,
 Hear me with patience but to speak a word.
CAPULET
 Hang thee, young baggage, disobedient wretch!
 I tell thee what: get thee to church o' Thursday
 Or never after look me in the face.
 Speak not, reply not, do not answer me!
 My fingers itch. Wife, we scarce thought us blest
 That God had lent us but this only child;
 But now I see this one is one too much,
 And that we have a curse in having her.
 Out on her, hilding!
NURSE   God in heaven bless her!   168
 You are to blame, my lord, to rate her so.   169
CAPULET
 And why, my Lady Wisdom? Hold your tongue,
 Good Prudence. Smatter with your gossips, go.   171
NURSE
 I speak no treason.
CAPULET   O, God-i'-good-e'en!   172
NURSE
 May not one speak?
CAPULET   Peace, you mumbling fool!
 Utter your gravity o'er a gossip's bowl,   174
 For here we need it not.
WIFE   You are too hot.

---

153 fettle make ready.   **'gainst** in anticipation of   **155 a hurdle** a conveyance on which criminals were dragged to execution   **156 greensickness**
(An anemic ailment of young unmarried women; it suggests Juliet's
paleness.)   **baggage** good-for-nothing   **157 tallow-face** pale-face
168 hilding worthless person   **169 rate** berate, scold   **171 Smatter** chat-
ter   **172 God-i'-good-e'en** i.e., for God's sake. (Literally, God give you good
evening.)   **174 gravity** wisdom. (Said contemptuously.)

CAPULET   God's bread, it makes me mad!   177
Day, night, hour, tide, time, work, play,   178
Alone, in company, still my care hath been
To have her matched. And having now provided
A gentleman of noble parentage,
Of fair demesnes, youthful, and nobly liened,   182
Stuffed, as they say, with honorable parts,   183
Proportioned as one's thought would wish a man—
And then to have a wretched puling fool,   185
A whining mammet, in her fortune's tender,   186
To answer, "I'll not wed, I cannot love,
I am too young; I pray you, pardon me."
But, an you will not wed, I'll pardon you.   189
Graze where you will, you shall not house with me.
Look to 't, think on 't. I do not use to jest.   191
Thursday is near. Lay hand on heart; advise.   192
An you be mine, I'll give you to my friend;
An you be not, hang, beg, starve, die in the streets,
For, by my soul, I'll ne'er acknowledge thee,
Nor what is mine shall never do thee good.
Trust to 't, bethink you. I'll not be forsworn.   *Exit.* 197
JULIET
Is there no pity sitting in the clouds
That sees into the bottom of my grief?
O sweet my Mother, cast me not away!
Delay this marriage for a month, a week;
Or if you do not, make the bridal bed
In that dim monument where Tybalt lies.
WIFE
Talk not to me, for I'll not speak a word.
Do as thou wilt, for I have done with thee.   *Exit.*
JULIET
O God!—O Nurse, how shall this be prevented?
My husband is on earth, my faith in heaven.   207

---

177 God's bread i.e., by God's (Christ's) Sacrament   **178 tide** season
182 demesnes estates.   **liened** descended   **183 parts** qualities
185 puling whining   **186 mammet** doll.   **in . . . tender** when an offer of
good fortune is made to her   **189 pardon you** i.e., allow you to depart.
(Said caustically.)   **191 do not use** am not accustomed   **192 advise**
consider carefully   **197 be forsworn** i.e., go back on my word   **207 my
faith in heaven** (Juliet refers to her marriage vows.)

How shall that faith return again to earth,   208
Unless that husband send it me from heaven   209
By leaving earth? Comfort me, counsel me.   210
Alack, alack, that heaven should practice stratagems 211
Upon so soft a subject as myself!
What sayst thou? Hast thou not a word of joy?
Some comfort, Nurse.

NURSE   Faith, here it is.
Romeo is banished, and all the world to nothing   215
That he dares ne'er come back to challenge you,   216
Or if he do, it needs must be by stealth.
Then, since the case so stands as now it doth,
I think it best you married with the County.
O, he's a lovely gentleman!
Romeo's a dishclout to him. An eagle, madam,   221
Hath not so green, so quick, so fair an eye   222
As Paris hath. Beshrew my very heart,   223
I think you are happy in this second match,
For it excels your first; or if it did not,
Your first is dead—or 'twere as good he were,
As living here and you no use of him.   227

JULIET   Speak'st thou from thy heart?

NURSE
And from my soul too. Else beshrew them both.

JULIET   Amen!   230

NURSE   What?

JULIET
Well, thou hast comforted me marvelous much.
Go in, and tell my lady I am gone,
Having displeased my father, to Laurence' cell
To make confession and to be absolved.

NURSE
Marry, I will; and this is wisely done.   [*Exit.*]

JULIET
Ancient damnation! O most wicked fiend!   237

208–210 How . . . leaving earth i.e., how can I remarry unless Romeo
dies   **211 practice** scheme, contrive   **215 all . . . nothing** the odds are
overwhelming   **216 challenge** lay claim to   **221 dishclout** dishrag
222 quick keen   **223 Beshrew** i.e., cursed be (also at l. 229)   **227 here**
i.e., on earth   **230 Amen** i.e., yes, indeed, *beshrew* (cursed be) your heart
and soul. (But Juliet does not explain this private meaning to the
Nurse.)   **237 Ancient damnation** damnable old woman

Is it more sin to wish me thus forsworn,   238
Or to dispraise my lord with that same tongue
Which she hath praised him with above compare
So many thousand times? Go, counselor,
Thou and my bosom henceforth shall be twain.   242
I'll to the Friar to know his remedy.
If all else fail, myself have power to die.   *Exit.*

✢

238 forsworn i.e., false to my marriage vows   **242 bosom** secret
thoughts.   **twain** separated

4.1   *Enter Friar [Laurence] and County Paris.*

FRIAR LAURENCE
  On Thursday, sir? The time is very short.
PARIS
  My father Capulet will have it so,
  And I am nothing slow to slack his haste.   3
FRIAR LAURENCE
  You say you do not know the lady's mind?
  Uneven is the course. I like it not.
PARIS
  Immoderately she weeps for Tybalt's death,
  And therefore have I little talked of love,
  For Venus smiles not in a house of tears.   8
  Now, sir, her father counts it dangerous
  That she do give her sorrow so much sway,
  And in his wisdom hastes our marriage   11
  To stop the inundation of her tears,
  Which, too much minded by herself alone,   13
  May be put from her by society.   14
  Now do you know the reason of this haste.
FRIAR LAURENCE [*Aside*]
  I would I knew not why it should be slowed.—
  Look, sir, here comes the lady toward my cell.

      Enter Juliet.

PARIS
  Happily met, my lady and my wife!
JULIET
  That may be, sir, when I may be a wife.
PARIS
  That "may be" must be, love, on Thursday next.
JULIET
  What must be shall be.
FRIAR LAURENCE   That's a certain text.

4.1. Location: Verona. Friar Laurence's cell.
3 nothing . . . haste not at all reluctant in a way that might slacken his
haste   **8 Venus . . . tears** (1) amorousness isn't appropriate in a house of
mourning (2) the planet Venus does not exert a favorable influence when
it is in an inauspicious *house* or portion of the zodiac   **11 hastes** hurries   **13 minded** thought about   **14 society** companionship

PARIS
Come you to make confession to this father?
JULIET
To answer that, I should confess to you.
PARIS
Do not deny to him that you love me.
JULIET
I will confess to you that I love him.
PARIS
So will ye, I am sure, that you love me.
JULIET
If I do so, it will be of more price,   27
Being spoke behind your back, than to your face.
PARIS
Poor soul, thy face is much abused with tears.
JULIET
The tears have got small victory by that,
For it was bad enough before their spite.   31
PARIS
Thou wrong'st it more than tears with that report.
JULIET
That is no slander, sir, which is a truth;
And what I spake, I spake it to my face.   34
PARIS
Thy face is mine, and thou hast slandered it.
JULIET
It may be so, for it is not mine own.—
Are you at leisure, holy Father, now,
Or shall I come to you at evening Mass?
FRIAR LAURENCE
My leisure serves me, pensive daughter, now.   39
My lord, we must entreat the time alone.   40
PARIS
God shield I should disturb devotion!   41
Juliet, on Thursday early will I rouse ye.
Till then, adieu, and keep this holy kiss.   *Exit.*
JULIET
O, shut the door! And when thou hast done so,
Come weep with me—past hope, past cure, past help!

27 more price greater worth   **31 spite** malice   **34 to my face** (1) openly
(2) about my face   **39 pensive** sorrowful   **40 entreat . . . alone** i.e., ask
you to leave us alone   **41 shield** prevent (that)

FRIAR LAURENCE
  Ah, Juliet, I already know thy grief;
  It strains me past the compass of my wits.   47
  I hear thou must, and nothing may prorogue it,   48
  On Thursday next be married to this county.
JULIET
  Tell me not, Friar, that thou hearest of this,
  Unless thou tell me how I may prevent it.
  If in thy wisdom thou canst give no help,
  Do thou but call my resolution wise
  And with this knife I'll help it presently.   54

                  [She shows a knife.]

  God joined my heart and Romeo's, thou our hands;
  And ere this hand, by thee to Romeo's sealed,
  Shall be the label to another deed,   57
  Or my true heart with treacherous revolt
  Turn to another, this shall slay them both.   59
  Therefore, out of thy long-experienced time,   60
  Give me some present counsel, or, behold,
  Twixt my extremes and me this bloody knife   62
  Shall play the umpire, arbitrating that
  Which the commission of thy years and art   64
  Could to no issue of true honor bring.
  Be not so long to speak; I long to die   66
  If what thou speak'st speak not of remedy.
FRIAR LAURENCE
  Hold, daughter. I do spy a kind of hope,
  Which craves as desperate an execution
  As that is desperate which we would prevent.
  If, rather than to marry County Paris,
  Thou hast the strength of will to slay thyself,
  Then is it likely thou wilt undertake
  A thing like death to chide away this shame,
  That cop'st with Death himself to scape from it;   75
  And if thou darest, I'll give thee remedy.

---

47 strains forces. **compass** bounds **48 may prorogue** can delay
54 presently at once **57 label** strip attached to a deed to carry the seal;
hence, confirmation, seal **59 both** i.e., hand and heart **60 time** age
62 extremes extreme difficulties **64 commission** authority. **art** skill
66 so long so slow **75 That cop'st** you who would encounter or negoti-
ate with; or, a thing that would cope. **it** i.e., shame

JULIET

O, bid me leap, rather than marry Paris,
From off the battlements of any tower,
Or walk in thievish ways, or bid me lurk   79
Where serpents are; chain me with roaring bears,
Or hide me nightly in a charnel house,   81
O'ercovered quite with dead men's rattling bones,
With reeky shanks and yellow chopless skulls;   83
Or bid me go into a new-made grave
And hide me with a dead man in his tomb—
Things that, to hear them told, have made me tremble—
And I will do it without fear or doubt,
To live an unstained wife to my sweet love.

FRIAR LAURENCE

Hold, then. Go home, be merry, give consent
To marry Paris. Wednesday is tomorrow.
Tomorrow night look that thou lie alone;
Let not the Nurse lie with thee in thy chamber.
Take thou this vial, being then in bed,
                        [*Showing her a vial*]
And this distilling liquor drink thou off,   94
When presently through all thy veins shall run
A cold and drowsy humor; for no pulse   96
Shall keep his native progress, but surcease;   97
No warmth, no breath shall testify thou livest;
The roses in thy lips and cheeks shall fade
To wanny ashes, thy eyes' windows fall   100
Like death when he shuts up the day of life;
Each part, deprived of supple government,   102
Shall, stiff and stark and cold, appear like death.
And in this borrowed likeness of shrunk death
Thou shalt continue two-and-forty hours,
And then awake as from a pleasant sleep.
Now, when the bridegroom in the morning comes
To rouse thee from thy bed, there art thou dead.
Then, as the manner of our country is,

---

79 thievish ways roads frequented by thieves   **81 charnel house** vault for human bones   **83 reeky** reeking, malodorous.   **chopless** without the lower jaw   **94 distilling** infusing   **96 humor** fluid, moisture   **97 his native** its natural.   **surcease** cease   **100 wanny** wan, pale   **102 supple government** control of motion

In thy best robes uncovered on the bier
Thou shalt be borne to that same ancient vault
Where all the kindred of the Capulets lie.
In the meantime, against thou shalt awake, 113
Shall Romeo by my letters know our drift, 114
And hither shall he come; and he and I
Will watch thy waking, and that very night
Shall Romeo bear thee hence to Mantua.
And this shall free thee from this present shame,
If no inconstant toy nor womanish fear 119
Abate thy valor in the acting it.

JULIET [*Taking the vial*]
Give me, give me! O, tell not me of fear!

FRIAR LAURENCE
Hold, get you gone. Be strong and prosperous 122
In this resolve. I'll send a friar with speed
To Mantua, with my letters to thy lord.

JULIET
Love give me strength, and strength shall help afford. 125
Farewell, dear Father!　　　　　*Exeunt [separately]*.

❧

4.2　　*Enter Father Capulet, Mother [Capulet's Wife],*
　　　　　Nurse, and Servingmen, two or three.

CAPULET
So many guests invite as here are writ.
　　　　　[*Exit one or two Servingmen.*]
Sirrah, go hire me twenty cunning cooks. 2

SERVINGMAN　You shall have none ill, sir, for I'll try 3
if they can lick their fingers.

CAPULET　How canst thou try them so?

SERVINGMAN　Marry, sir, 'tis an ill cook that cannot
lick his own fingers; therefore he that cannot lick his
fingers goes not with me.

CAPULET　Go, begone.　　　　　[*Exit Servingman.*]

---

113 against anticipating when　**114 drift** plan　**119 toy** idle fancy
122 prosperous successful　**125 help afford** provide help

4.2. Location: Verona. Capulet's house.
2 cunning skilled　**3 none ill** no bad ones.　**try** test

We shall be much unfurnished for this time.   10
What, is my daughter gone to Friar Laurence?

NURSE   Ay, forsooth.

CAPULET
Well, he may chance to do some good on her.
A peevish self-willed harlotry it is.   14

Enter Juliet.

NURSE
See where she comes from shrift with merry look.

CAPULET
How now, my headstrong, where have you been
    gadding?   16

JULIET
Where I have learned me to repent the sin
Of disobedient opposition
To you and your behests, and am enjoined   19
By holy Laurence to fall prostrate here,   [*Kneeling*]
To beg your pardon. Pardon, I beseech you!
Henceforward I am ever ruled by you.

CAPULET
Send for the County! Go tell him of this.
I'll have this knot knit up tomorrow morning.

JULIET
I met the youthful lord at Laurence' cell
And gave him what becomèd love I might,   26
Not stepping o'er the bounds of modesty.

CAPULET
Why, I am glad on 't. This is well. Stand up.
                                  [*Juliet rises.*]
This is as 't should be. Let me see the County;
Ay, marry, go, I say, and fetch him hither.
Now, afore God, this reverend holy friar,
All our whole city is much bound to him.   32

JULIET
Nurse, will you go with me into my closet   33
To help me sort such needful ornaments   34
As you think fit to furnish me tomorrow?

---

10 unfurnished unprovided   **14 A peevish . . . is** i.e., she's a silly good-for-
nothing   **16 gadding** wandering   **19 behests** commands   **26 becomèd**
befitting   **32 bound** indebted   **33 closet** chamber   **34 sort** choose

WIFE
 No, not till Thursday. There is time enough.
CAPULET
 Go, Nurse, go with her. We'll to church tomorrow.
 Exeunt [Juliet and Nurse].

WIFE
 We shall be short in our provision.
 'Tis now near night.
CAPULET Tush, I will stir about,
 And all things shall be well, I warrant thee, wife.
 Go thou to Juliet, help to deck up her. 41
 I'll not to bed tonight. Let me alone.
 I'll play the huswife for this once.—What ho!— 43
 They are all forth. Well, I will walk myself
 To County Paris, to prepare up him
 Against tomorrow. My heart is wondrous light,
 Since this same wayward girl is so reclaimed.
 Exeunt.

❧

4.3 *Enter Juliet and Nurse.*

JULIET
 Ay, those attires are best. But, gentle Nurse,
 I pray thee, leave me to myself tonight;
 For I have need of many orisons 3
 To move the heavens to smile upon my state,
 Which, well thou knowest, is cross and full of sin. 5

 Enter Mother [Capulet's Wife].

WIFE
 What, are you busy, ho? Need you my help?
JULIET
 No, madam, we have culled such necessaries 7
 As are behooveful for our state tomorrow. 8
 So please you, let me now be left alone,

---

41 deck up dress, adorn **43 huswife** housewife

4.3. Location: Verona. Capulet's house; Juliet's bed, enclosed by bedcurtains, is thrust out or is otherwise visible.
3 orisons prayers **5 cross** contrary, perverse **7 culled** picked out
8 behooveful needful. **state** ceremony

And let the Nurse this night sit up with you,
For I am sure you have your hands full all
In this so sudden business.
WIFE   Good night.
Get thee to bed and rest, for thou hast need.
                    Exeunt [Capulet's Wife and Nurse].

JULIET
Farewell! God knows when we shall meet again.
I have a faint cold fear thrills through my veins   15
That almost freezes up the heat of life.
I'll call them back again to comfort me.
Nurse!—What should she do here?
My dismal scene I needs must act alone.
Come, vial.   *[She takes out the vial.]*
What if this mixture do not work at all?
Shall I be married then tomorrow morning?
No, no, this shall forbid it. Lie thou there.
                    [She lays down a dagger.]
What if it be a poison which the Friar
Subtly hath ministered to have me dead,
Lest in this marriage he should be dishonored
Because he married me before to Romeo?
I fear it is; and yet methinks it should not,
For he hath still been tried a holy man.   29
How if, when I am laid into the tomb,
I wake before the time that Romeo
Come to redeem me? There's a fearful point!
Shall I not then be stifled in the vault,
To whose foul mouth no healthsome air breathes in,
And there die strangled ere my Romeo comes?
Or, if I live, is it not very like,   36
The horrible conceit of death and night,   37
Together with the terror of the place—
As in a vault, an ancient receptacle,   39
Where for this many hundred years the bones
Of all my buried ancestors are packed;
Where bloody Tybalt, yet but green in earth,   42

---

15 faint producing faintness. **thrills** pierces, shivers **29 still** always.
tried proved **36 like** likely (also at l. 45) **37 conceit** idea **39 As**
namely **42 green** new, freshly

Lies festering in his shroud; where, as they say,
At some hours in the night spirits resort—
Alack, alack, is it not like that I,
So early waking, what with loathsome smells,
And shrieks like mandrakes torn out of the earth,   47
That living mortals, hearing them, run mad—   48
O, if I wake, shall I not be distraught,
Environèd with all these hideous fears,   50
And madly play with my forefathers' joints,
And pluck the mangled Tybalt from his shroud,
And in this rage, with some great kinsman's bone   53
As with a club dash out my desperate brains?
O, look! Methinks I see my cousin's ghost
Seeking out Romeo, that did spit his body   56
Upon a rapier's point. Stay, Tybalt, stay!   57
Romeo, Romeo, Romeo! Here's drink—I drink to thee.
                    [*She drinks and falls upon her bed,*
                                within the curtains.]

4.4   *Enter Lady of the House [Capulet's Wife] and*
            Nurse.

WIFE
  Hold, take these keys, and fetch more spices, Nurse.
NURSE
  They call for dates and quinces in the pastry.   2

        Enter old Capulet.

CAPULET
  Come, stir, stir, stir! The second cock hath crowed.
  The curfew bell hath rung; 'tis three o'clock.
  Look to the baked meats, good Angelica.   5
  Spare not for cost.

47 mandrakes (The root of the mandragora or mandrake resembled the
human form; the plant was fabled to utter a shriek when torn from the
ground.)   **48 That** so that   **50 fears** objects of fear   **53 rage** madness.
great i.e., of an earlier generation, as in *great*-grandfather   **56 spit**
impale   **57 Stay** stop

4.4. Location: Scene continues. Juliet's bed remains visible.
2 pastry room in which pastry was made   **5 baked meats** pies, pastry

NURSE   Go, you cotquean, go,   6
  Get you to bed. Faith, you'll be sick tomorrow
  For this night's watching.   8
CAPULET
  No, not a whit. What, I have watched ere now
  All night for lesser cause, and ne'er been sick.
WIFE
  Ay, you have been a mouse-hunt in your time,   11
  But I will watch you from such watching now.   12
                            Exeunt Lady and Nurse.
CAPULET A jealous hood, a jealous hood!   13

        *Enter three or four [Servingmen] with spits and
        logs, and baskets.*

  Now, fellow, what is there?
FIRST SERVINGMAN
  Things for the cook, sir, but I know not what.
CAPULET
  Make haste, make haste. [*Exit First Servingman.*] Sir-
    rah, fetch drier logs.
  Call Peter. He will show thee where they are.
SECOND SERVINGMAN
  I have a head, sir, that will find out logs
  And never trouble Peter for the matter.
CAPULET
  Mass, and well said. A merry whoreson, ha!   20
  Thou shalt be loggerhead. [*Exit Servingman.*] Good
    faith, 'tis day.   21
  The County will be here with music straight,   22
  For so he said he would. I hear him near.
                            Play music [within].
  Nurse! Wife! What ho! What, Nurse, I say!

        Enter Nurse.

  Go waken Juliet, go and trim her up.   25

6 cotquean i.e., a man who acts the housewife. (Literally, a cottage
housewife.) **8 watching** being awake **11 mouse-hunt** i.e., hunter of
women **12 watch . . . watching** i.e., keep an eye on you to prevent such
nighttime activity **13 A jealous hood** i.e., you wear the cap of jeal-
ousy **20 Mass** by the Mass. **whoreson** i.e., fellow. (An abusive term
used familiarly.) **21 loggerhead** (1) put in charge of getting logs (2) a
blockhead **22 straight** straightway, immediately **25 trim** dress

I'll go and chat with Paris. Hie, make haste,
Make haste. The bridegroom he is come already.
Make haste, I say.   [*Exit Capulet.*]

4.5   [*The Nurse goes to the bed.*]

NURSE
Mistress! What, mistress! Juliet! Fast, I warrant her,
    she.   1
Why, lamb, why, lady! Fie, you slugabed!
Why, love, I say! Madam! Sweetheart! Why, bride!
What, not a word? You take your pennyworths now.   4
Sleep for a week; for the next night, I warrant,
The County Paris hath set up his rest   6
That you shall rest but little. God forgive me,
Marry, and amen! How sound is she asleep!
I needs must wake her. Madam, madam, madam!
Ay, let the County take you in your bed;
He'll fright you up, i' faith. Will it not be?
                    [*She opens the bedcurtains.*]
What, dressed, and in your clothes, and down again?
I must needs wake you. Lady, lady, lady!
Alas, alas! Help, help! My lady's dead!
O, weraday, that ever I was born!   15
Some aqua vitae, ho! My lord! My lady!   16

        [*Enter Capulet's Wife.*]

WIFE
What noise is here?
NURSE   O lamentable day!
WIFE
What is the matter?
NURSE   Look, look! O heavy day!   18
WIFE
O me, O me! My child, my only life!

4.5. Location: Scene continues. Juliet's bed remains visible.
1 Fast fast asleep   **4 pennyworths** small portions (of sleep)   **6 set up his
rest** firmly resolved. (From primero, a card game, where it means "staked
his reserve." The Nurse speaks bawdily.)   **15 weraday** wellaway, alas
16 aqua vitae strong alcoholic spirits   **18 heavy** sorrowful

Revive, look up, or I will die with thee!
Help, help! Call help.

Enter Father [Capulet].

CAPULET
For shame, bring Juliet forth. Her lord is come.
NURSE
She's dead, deceased. She's dead, alack the day!
WIFE
Alack the day, she's dead, she's dead, she's dead!
CAPULET
Ha! Let me see her. Out, alas! She's cold.
Her blood is settled, and her joints are stiff;   26
Life and these lips have long been separated.
Death lies on her like an untimely frost
Upon the sweetest flower of all the field.
NURSE
O lamentable day!
WIFE   O woeful time!
CAPULET
Death, that hath ta'en her hence to make me wail,
Ties up my tongue and will not let me speak.

*Enter Friar [Laurence] and the County [Paris,
with Musicians].*

FRIAR LAURENCE
Come, is the bride ready to go to church?
CAPULET
Ready to go, but never to return.
O son, the night before thy wedding day
Hath Death lain with thy wife. There she lies,
Flower as she was, deflowered by him.
Death is my son-in-law, Death is my heir;
My daughter he hath wedded. I will die
And leave him all; life, living, all is Death's.   40
PARIS
Have I thought long to see this morning's face,   41
And doth it give me such a sight as this?

26 settled congealed   **40 living** means of living, property   **41 thought
long** looked forward to

WIFE
Accurst, unhappy, wretched, hateful day!   43
Most miserable hour that e'er time saw
In lasting labor of his pilgrimage!   45
But one, poor one, one poor and loving child,
But one thing to rejoice and solace in,
And cruel Death hath catched it from my sight!   48

NURSE
O woe! O woeful, woeful, woeful day!
Most lamentable day, most woeful day
That ever, ever I did yet behold!
O day, O day, O day! O hateful day!
Never was seen so black a day as this.
O woeful day, O woeful day!

PARIS
Beguiled, divorcèd, wrongèd, spited, slain!   55
Most detestable Death, by thee beguiled,
By cruel, cruel thee quite overthrown!
O love! O life! Not life, but love in death!

CAPULET
Despised, distressèd, hated, martyred, killed!
Uncomfortable time, why cam'st thou now   60
To murder, murder our solemnity?   61
O child! O child! My soul, and not my child!
Dead art thou! Alack, my child is dead,
And with my child my joys are buried.

FRIAR LAURENCE
Peace, ho, for shame! Confusion's cure lives not   65
In these confusions. Heaven and yourself
Had part in this fair maid; now heaven hath all,
And all the better is it for the maid.
Your part in her you could not keep from death,   69
But heaven keeps his part in eternal life.
The most you sought was her promotion,   71
For 'twas your heaven she should be advanced;   72
And weep ye now, seeing she is advanced
Above the clouds, as high as heaven itself?

---

43 unhappy fatal   **45 lasting** unceasing   **48 catched** snatched
55 Beguiled cheated   **60 Uncomfortable** comfortless   **61 solemnity**
ceremony, festivity   **65 Confusion's** calamity's   **69 Your part** i.e., the
mortal part   **71 promotion** social advancement   **72 your heaven** i.e.,
your idea of the greatest good

O, in this love you love your child so ill
That you run mad, seeing that she is well.
She's not well married that lives married long,
But she's best married that dies married young.
Dry up your tears, and stick your rosemary   79
On this fair corpse, and, as the custom is,
And in her best array, bear her to church;
For though fond nature bids us all lament,   82
Yet nature's tears are reason's merriment.   83

CAPULET
All things that we ordainèd festival   84
Turn from their office to black funeral: 85
Our instruments to melancholy bells,
Our wedding cheer to a sad burial feast,
Our solemn hymns to sullen dirges change,   88
Our bridal flowers serve for a buried corpse,
And all things change them to the contrary.   90

FRIAR LAURENCE
Sir, go you in, and, madam, go with him,
And go, Sir Paris. Everyone prepare
To follow this fair corpse unto her grave.
The heavens do lour upon you for some ill;   94
Move them no more by crossing their high will.   95
                    Exeunt. Manet [Nurse with Musicians].

FIRST MUSICIAN
Faith, we may put up our pipes and be gone.

NURSE
Honest good fellows, ah, put up, put up!
For well you know this is a pitiful case.   [*Exit.*]

FIRST MUSICIAN
Ay, by my troth, the case may be amended.   99

---

79 rosemary symbol of immortality and enduring love; therefore used at
both funerals and weddings   **82 fond nature** foolish human nature
83 nature's . . . merriment that which causes human nature to weep is
an occasion of joy to reason   **84 ordainèd festival** intended to be fes-
tive   **85 office** function   **88 sullen** mournful   **90 them** themselves
94 lour threaten.   **for some ill** on account of some sin   **95 Move** i.e.,
anger   **s.d. Manet** she remains onstage   **99 case . . . amended**
(1) things generally could be much better (2) the instrument case could
be repaired

Enter Peter.

PETER Musicians, O, musicians, "Heart's ease," 100
"Heart's ease." O, an you will have me live, play
"Heart's ease."

FIRST MUSICIAN Why "Heart's ease"?

PETER O, musicians, because my heart itself plays "My 104
heart is full." O, play me some merry dump to comfort 105
me.

FIRST MUSICIAN Not a dump we! 'Tis no time to play
now.

PETER You will not, then?

FIRST MUSICIAN No.

PETER I will then give it you soundly.

FIRST MUSICIAN What will you give us?

PETER No money, on my faith, but the gleek; I will give 113
you the minstrel. 114

FIRST MUSICIAN Then will I give you the serving-creature.

PETER Then will I lay the serving-creature's dagger on
your pate. I will carry no crotchets. I'll re you, I'll fa you. 118
Do you note me? 119

FIRST MUSICIAN An you re us and fa us, you note us.

SECOND MUSICIAN Pray you, put up your dagger and
put out your wit. 122

PETER Then have at you with my wit! I will dry-beat 123
you with an iron wit, and put up my iron dagger. An-
swer me like men:
"When griping griefs the heart doth wound, 126
And doleful dumps the mind oppress,
Then music with her silver sound"— 128

---

s.d. Enter Peter (The second quarto has *Enter Will Kemp*, well-known comic actor and member of Shakespeare's company, for whom Shakespeare evidently intended this role and so named him in the manuscript.)
100, 104–105 "Heart's ease," "My heart is full" (Popular ballads.)
105 dump mournful tune or dance **113 gleek** jest, gibe **113–114 give you the minstrel** insultingly term you a minstrel, i.e., vagabond
118 carry no crotchets (1) endure no whims (2) sing no quarter notes.
re, fa musical notes **119 note** (1) heed (2) set to music **122 put out** display **123 dry-beat** thrash (without drawing blood) **126–128 "When . . . sound"** (From Richard Edwards's song "In Commendation of Music," published in *The Paradise of Dainty Devices*, 1576.)

Why "silver sound"? Why "music with her silver
sound"? What say you, Simon Catling?   130
FIRST MUSICIAN   Marry, sir, because silver hath a sweet
sound.
PETER   Pretty! What say you, Hugh Rebeck?   133
SECOND MUSICIAN   I say "silver sound" because musi-
cians sound for silver.   135
PETER   Pretty too! What say you, James Soundpost?   136
THIRD MUSICIAN   Faith, I know not what to say.
PETER   O, I cry you mercy, you are the singer. I will say 138
for you. It is "music with her silver sound" because
musicians have no gold for sounding: 140
        "Then music with her silver sound
        With speedy help doth lend redress."   *Exit.*
FIRST MUSICIAN   What a pestilent knave is this same!
SECOND MUSICIAN   Hang him, Jack! Come, we'll in here,
tarry for the mourners, and stay dinner.   *Exeunt.* 145

✛

130 **Catling** (A catling was a small lutestring made of catgut.)
133 **Rebeck** (A rebeck was a fiddle with three strings.)   135 **sound** make
music   136 **Soundpost** (A soundpost is the pillar or peg that supports
the sounding board of a stringed instrument.)   138 **cry you mercy** beg
your pardon   140 **have . . . sounding** i.e., are paid only silver for playing   145 **stay** await

5.1 *Enter Romeo.*

ROMEO

If I may trust the flattering truth of sleep,   1
My dreams presage some joyful news at hand.
My bosom's lord sits lightly in his throne,   3
And all this day an unaccustomed spirit
Lifts me above the ground with cheerful thoughts.
I dreamt my lady came and found me dead—
Strange dream that gives a dead man leave to think!—
And breathed such life with kisses in my lips
That I revived and was an emperor.
Ah me, how sweet is love itself possessed   10
When but love's shadows are so rich in joy!   11

    Enter Romeo's man [*Balthasar, booted*].

News from Verona! How now, Balthasar,
Dost thou not bring me letters from the Friar?
How doth my lady? Is my father well?
How fares my Juliet? That I ask again,
For nothing can be ill if she be well.

BALTHASAR

Then she is well, and nothing can be ill.
Her body sleeps in Capels' monument,
And her immortal part with angels lives.
I saw her laid low in her kindred's vault
And presently took post to tell it you.   21
O, pardon me for bringing these ill news,
Since you did leave it for my office, sir.   23

ROMEO

Is it e'en so? Then I defy you, stars!
Thou knowest my lodging. Get me ink and paper,
And hire post-horses. I will hence tonight.

BALTHASAR

I do beseech you, sir, have patience.

5.1. Location: Mantua. A street.
1 flattering favorable (but potentially illusory)   **3 bosom's lord** i.e.,
heart   **10 itself possessed** actually enjoyed   **11 shadows** dreams
s.d. booted wearing riding boots—a conventional stage sign of traveling
21 presently took post at once started off in haste; or, with post-
horses   **23 office** duty

Your looks are pale and wild, and do import   28
Some misadventure.
ROMEO   Tush, thou art deceived.
Leave me, and do the thing I bid thee do.
Hast thou no letters to me from the Friar?
BALTHASAR
No, my good lord.
ROMEO   No matter. Get thee gone,
And hire those horses. I'll be with thee straight.
                                    Exit [*Balthasar*].
Well, Juliet, I will lie with thee tonight.
Let's see for means. O mischief, thou art swift   35
To enter in the thoughts of desperate men!
I do remember an apothecary—   37
And hereabouts 'a dwells—which late I noted   38
In tattered weeds, with overwhelming brows,   39
Culling of simples. Meager were his looks;   40
Sharp misery had worn him to the bones;
And in his needy shop a tortoise hung,
An alligator stuffed, and other skins
Of ill-shaped fishes; and about his shelves
A beggarly account of empty boxes,   45
Green earthen pots, bladders, and musty seeds,
Remnants of packthread, and old cakes of roses   47
Were thinly scattered to make up a show.
Noting this penury, to myself I said,
"An if a man did need a poison now,   50
Whose sale is present death in Mantua,   51
Here lives a caitiff wretch would sell it him."   52
O, this same thought did but forerun my need,
And this same needy man must sell it me.
As I remember, this should be the house.
Being holiday, the beggar's shop is shut.
What, ho! Apothecary!

        [*Enter Apothecary.*]

---

28 import signify   **35 for means** by what means   **37 apothecary** drug-
gist   **38 which . . . noted** whom lately I noticed   **39 weeds** garments.
overwhelming brows eyebrows jutting out over his eyes   **40 simples**
medicinal herbs.   **Meager** impoverished   **45 beggarly account** poor
array   **47 cakes of roses** petals pressed into cakes to be used as per-
fume   **50 An if** if   **51 present** immediate   **52 caitiff** miserable.   **would**
who would

APOTHECARY   Who calls so loud?

ROMEO

Come hither, man. I see that thou art poor.
Hold, there is forty ducats. [*He shows gold.*] Let me have 59
A dram of poison, such soon-speeding gear   60
As will disperse itself through all the veins
That the life-weary taker may fall dead,
And that the trunk may be discharged of breath   63
As violently as hasty powder fired
Doth hurry from the fatal cannon's womb.

APOTHECARY

Such mortal drugs I have, but Mantua's law   66
Is death to any he that utters them.   67

ROMEO

Art thou so bare and full of wretchedness,
And fearest to die? Famine is in thy cheeks,
Need and oppression starveth in thy eyes,   70
Contempt and beggary hangs upon thy back.
The world is not thy friend, nor the world's law;
The world affords no law to make thee rich.
Then be not poor, but break it, and take this.

APOTHECARY

My poverty but not my will consents.

ROMEO

I pay thy poverty and not thy will.

APOTHECARY

Put this in any liquid thing you will
And drink it off, and if you had the strength
Of twenty men it would dispatch you straight.
         [*He gives poison, and takes the gold.*]

ROMEO

There is thy gold—worse poison to men's souls,
Doing more murder in this loathsome world
Than these poor compounds that thou mayst not sell.
I sell thee poison; thou hast sold me none.
Farewell. Buy food, and get thyself in flesh.—
Come, cordial and not poison, go with me   85

---

59 ducats gold coins   **60 soon-speeding gear** quickly effective stuff
63 trunk body   **66 mortal** deadly   **67 any he** anyone. **utters** issues,
gives out   **70 starveth** are revealed by the starving look   **85 cordial**
restorative for the heart

To Juliet's grave, for there must I use thee.

Exeunt [separately].

✛

5.2   *Enter Friar John to Friar Laurence.*

FRIAR JOHN
  Holy Franciscan friar! Brother, ho!

  Enter [Friar] Laurence.

FRIAR LAURENCE
  This same should be the voice of Friar John.
  Welcome from Mantua! What says Romeo?
  Or if his mind be writ, give me his letter.   4

FRIAR JOHN
  Going to find a barefoot brother out—
  One of our order—to associate me   6
  Here in this city visiting the sick,
  And finding him, the searchers of the town,   8
  Suspecting that we both were in a house
  Where the infectious pestilence did reign,
  Sealed up the doors and would not let us forth,
  So that my speed to Mantua there was stayed.   12

FRIAR LAURENCE
  Who bare my letter, then, to Romeo?

FRIAR JOHN
  I could not send it—here it is again—
  Nor get a messenger to bring it thee,
  So fearful were they of infection.   *[He gives a letter.]*

FRIAR LAURENCE
  Unhappy fortune! By my brotherhood,
  The letter was not nice but full of charge,   18
  Of dear import, and the neglecting it   19

5.2. **Location: Verona. Friar Laurence's cell.**
4 mind thoughts **6 associate** accompany **8 searchers of the town**
town officials charged with public health (and especially concerned
about the *pestilence* or plague) **12 speed** successful journey,
progress. **stayed** prevented **18 nice** trivial. **charge** importance
19 dear precious, urgent

May do much danger. Friar John, go hence.
Get me an iron crow and bring it straight   21
Unto my cell.

FRIAR JOHN   Brother, I'll go and bring it thee.   *Exit.*

FRIAR LAURENCE
Now must I to the monument alone.
Within this three hours will fair Juliet wake.
She will beshrew me much that Romeo   26
Hath had no notice of these accidents;   27
But I will write again to Mantua,
And keep her at my cell till Romeo come—
Poor living corpse, closed in a dead man's tomb! *Exit.*

✤

5.3   *Enter Paris, and his Page [bearing flowers,
perfumed water, and a torch].*

PARIS
Give me thy torch, boy. Hence, and stand aloof.   1
Yet put it out, for I would not be seen.
Under yond yew trees lay thee all along,   3
Holding thy ear close to the hollow ground.
So shall no foot upon the churchyard tread,
Being loose, unfirm, with digging up of graves,   6
But thou shalt hear it. Whistle then to me
As signal that thou hearest something approach.
Give me those flowers. Do as I bid thee. Go.

PAGE *[Aside]*
I am almost afraid to stand alone
Here in the churchyard, yet I will adventure.
                                        [He retires.]

PARIS *[Strewing flowers and perfumed water]*
Sweet flower, with flowers thy bridal bed I strew—
O woe! Thy canopy is dust and stones—   13

---

21 crow crowbar   **26 beshrew** i.e., reprove   **27 accidents** events

**5.3. Location: Verona. A churchyard and the vault or tomb belonging to
the Capulets.**
1 aloof to one side, at a distance   **3 all along** at full length   **6 Being** i.e.,
the soil being   **13 canopy** covering

Which with sweet water nightly I will dew,   14
  Or wanting that, with tears distilled by moans.   15
The obsequies that I for thee will keep   16
Nightly shall be to strew thy grave and weep.

                      Whistle Boy.

The boy gives warning something doth approach.
What cursèd foot wanders this way tonight,
To cross my obsequies and true love's rite?   20
What, with a torch? Muffle me, night, awhile.   21

                         [He retires.]

   Enter Romeo and [Balthasar, with a torch, a
   mattock, and a crowbar].

ROMEO
Give me that mattock and the wrenching iron.   22

                 [He takes the tools.]

Hold, take this letter. Early in the morning
See thou deliver it to my lord and father.

       [He gives a letter and takes a torch.]

Give me the light. Upon thy life I charge thee,
Whate'er thou hearest or seest, stand all aloof
And do not interrupt me in my course.   27
Why I descend into this bed of death
Is partly to behold my lady's face,
But chiefly to take thence from her dead finger
A precious ring—a ring that I must use
In dear employment. Therefore hence, begone.   32
But if thou, jealous, dost return to pry   33
In what I farther shall intend to do,
By heaven, I will tear thee joint by joint
And strew this hungry churchyard with thy limbs.
The time and my intents are savage-wild,
More fierce and more inexorable far
Than empty tigers or the roaring sea.   39

BALTHASAR
I will be gone, sir, and not trouble ye.

14 **dew** moisten   15 **wanting** lacking   16 **obsequies** ceremonies in
memory of the dead   20 **cross** interrupt   21 **Muffle** conceal
s.d. mattock pickax   22 **wrenching iron** crowbar   27 **course** intended
action   32 **dear employment** important business   33 **jealous** suspi-
cious   39 **empty** hungry

ROMEO
> So shalt thou show me friendship. Take thou that.
>> [*He gives him money.*]
> Live, and be prosperous; and farewell, good fellow.

BALTHASAR [*Aside*]
> For all this same, I'll hide me hereabout.   43
> His looks I fear, and his intents I doubt.   [*He retires.*] 44

ROMEO
> Thou detestable maw, thou womb of death,   45
> Gorged with the dearest morsel of the earth,
> Thus I enforce thy rotten jaws to open,
> And in despite I'll cram thee with more food.   48
>> [*He begins to open the tomb.*]

PARIS
> This is that banished haughty Montague
> That murdered my love's cousin, with which grief
> It is supposèd the fair creature died,
> And here is come to do some villainous shame
> To the dead bodies. I will apprehend him.
>> [*He comes forward.*]
> Stop thy unhallowed toil, vile Montague!
> Can vengeance be pursued further than death?
> Condemnèd villain, I do apprehend thee.
> Obey and go with me, for thou must die.

ROMEO
> I must indeed, and therefore came I hither.
> Good gentle youth, tempt not a desperate man.
> Fly hence and leave me. Think upon these gone;   60
> Let them affright thee. I beseech thee, youth,
> Put not another sin upon my head
> By urging me to fury. O, begone!
> By heaven, I love thee better than myself,
> For I come hither armed against myself.
> Stay not, begone. Live, and hereafter say
> A madman's mercy bid thee run away.

PARIS
> I do defy thy conjuration,
> And apprehend thee for a felon here.

---

43 For all this same all the same   **44 doubt** suspect   **45 womb** belly
48 in despite defiantly   **60 gone** dead

ROMEO
Wilt thou provoke me? Then have at thee, boy!
[They fight.]

PAGE
O Lord, they fight! I will go call the watch.   [Exit.]

PARIS
O, I am slain! [He falls.] If thou be merciful,
Open the tomb, lay me with Juliet.   [He dies.]

ROMEO
In faith, I will. Let me peruse this face.
Mercutio's kinsman, noble County Paris!
What said my man when my betossèd soul
Did not attend him as we rode? I think
He told me Paris should have married Juliet.
Said he not so? Or did I dream it so?
Or am I mad, hearing him talk of Juliet,
To think it was so? O, give me thy hand,
One writ with me in sour misfortune's book.
I'll bury thee in a triumphant grave.
[He opens the tomb.]
A grave? O, no! A lantern, slaughtered youth,   84
For here lies Juliet, and her beauty makes
This vault a feasting presence full of light.   86
Death, lie thou there, by a dead man interred.
[He lays Paris in the tomb.]
How oft when men are at the point of death
Have they been merry, which their keepers call   89
A lightening before death! O, how may I   90
Call this a lightening? O my love, my wife!
Death, that hath sucked the honey of thy breath,
Hath had no power yet upon thy beauty.
Thou art not conquered; beauty's ensign yet   94
Is crimson in thy lips and in thy cheeks,
And death's pale flag is not advancèd there.   96
Tybalt, liest thou there in thy bloody sheet?   97
O, what more favor can I do to thee
Than with that hand that cut thy youth in twain

---

84 lantern turret room full of windows **86 feasting presence** reception chamber for feasting **89 keepers** attendants **90 lightening** exhilaration (supposed to occur just before death) **94 ensign** banner **96 advancèd** raised **97 sheet** shroud

To sunder his that was thine enemy?   100
Forgive me, cousin! Ah, dear Juliet,
Why art thou yet so fair? Shall I believe
That unsubstantial Death is amorous,   103
And that the lean abhorrèd monster keeps
Thee here in dark to be his paramour?
For fear of that I still will stay with thee   106
And never from this palace of dim night
Depart again. Here, here will I remain
With worms that are thy chambermaids. O, here
Will I set up my everlasting rest   110
And shake the yoke of inauspicious stars
From this world-wearied flesh. Eyes, look your last!
Arms, take your last embrace! And, lips, O you
The doors of breath, seal with a righteous kiss
A dateless bargain to engrossing death!   115
                    [*He kisses Juliet.*]
Come, bitter conduct, come, unsavory guide,   116
Thou desperate pilot, now at once run on   117
The dashing rocks thy seasick weary bark!
Here's to my love. [*He drinks.*] O true apothecary!
Thy drugs are quick. Thus with a kiss I die. [*He dies.*]

        Enter [at the other end of the churchyard] Friar
        [Laurence] with lantern, crow, and spade.

FRIAR LAURENCE
Saint Francis be my speed! How oft tonight   121
Have my old feet stumbled at graves! Who's there?
BALTHASAR
Here's one, a friend, and one that knows you well.
FRIAR LAURENCE
Bliss be upon you. Tell me, good my friend,
What torch is yond that vainly lends his light   125
To grubs and eyeless skulls? As I discern,   126
It burneth in the Capels' monument.

100 **his** i.e., my (Romeo's) own   103 **unsubstantial** lacking material exis-
tence   106 **still** always   110 **set . . . rest** (See 4.5.6. The meaning is,
"make my final determination," with allusion to the idea of repose.)
115 **dateless bargain** everlasting contract.   **engrossing** monopolizing,
taking all; also, drawing up the contract   116 **conduct** guide (i.e., the
poison)   117 **desperate** reckless, despairing   121 **be my speed** prosper
me   125 **vainly** uselessly   126 **grubs** insect larvae

BALTHASAR
  It doth so, holy sir, and there's my master,
  One that you love.
FRIAR LAURENCE   Who is it?
BALTHASAR   Romeo.
FRIAR LAURENCE
  How long hath he been there?
BALTHASAR   Full half an hour.
FRIAR LAURENCE
  Go with me to the vault.
BALTHASAR   I dare not, sir.
  My master knows not but I am gone hence,
  And fearfully did menace me with death
  If I did stay to look on his intents.
FRIAR LAURENCE
  Stay, then, I'll go alone. Fear comes upon me.
  O, much I fear some ill unthrifty thing.   .136
BALTHASAR
  As I did sleep under this yew tree here
  I dreamt my master and another fought,
  And that my master slew him.
FRIAR LAURENCE [*Advancing to the tomb*] Romeo!
  Alack, alack, what blood is this which stains
  The stony entrance of this sepulcher?
  What mean these masterless and gory swords
  To lie discolored by this place of peace?
                              [*He enters the tomb.*]
  Romeo! O, pale! Who else? What, Paris too?
  And steeped in blood? Ah, what an unkind hour   145
  Is guilty of this lamentable chance!
  The lady stirs.   [*Juliet wakes.*]
JULIET
  O comfortable Friar, where is my lord?   148
  I do remember well where I should be,
  And there I am. Where is my Romeo? [*A noise within.*]
FRIAR LAURENCE
  I hear some noise. Lady, come from that nest
  Of death, contagion, and unnatural sleep.
  A greater power than we can contradict

136 unthrifty unfortunate   **145 unkind** unnatural   **148 comfortable**
comforting

Hath thwarted our intents. Come, come away.
Thy husband in thy bosom there lies dead,
And Paris, too. Come, I'll dispose of thee
Among a sisterhood of holy nuns.
Stay not to question, for the watch is coming.
Come, go, good Juliet. [*A noise again.*] I dare no longer
    stay.   *Exit* [*Friar Laurence*].

JULIET
Go, get thee hence, for I will not away.
What's here? A cup, closed in my true love's hand?
Poison, I see, hath been his timeless end.   162
O churl, drunk all, and left no friendly drop   163
To help me after? I will kiss thy lips;
Haply some poison yet doth hang on them,   165
To make me die with a restorative.   [*She kisses him.*]
Thy lips are warm.

> *Enter* [*Paris's*] *Boy and Watch* [*at the other end of*
> *the churchyard*].

FIRST WATCH   Lead, boy. Which way?
JULIET
Yea, noise? Then I'll be brief. O happy dagger!   169
                          [*She takes Romeo's dagger.*]
This is thy sheath. There rust, and let me die.
                          [*She stabs herself and falls.*]
PAGE
This is the place, there where the torch doth burn.
FIRST WATCH
The ground is bloody. Search about the churchyard.
Go, some of you, whoe'er you find attach.   173
                          [*Exeunt some.*]
Pitiful sight! Here lies the County slain,
And Juliet bleeding, warm, and newly dead, ——
Who here hath lain this two days buried.
Go tell the Prince. Run to the Capulets.
Raise up the Montagues. Some others search.
                          [*Exeunt others.*]
We see the ground whereon these woes do lie,

162 **timeless** (1) untimely (2) everlasting   163 **churl** miser   165 **Haply**
perhaps   169 **happy** opportune   173 **attach** arrest, detain

But the true ground of all these piteous woes   180
We cannot without circumstance descry.   181

    Enter [some of the Watch, with] Romeo's man
    [Balthasar].

SECOND WATCH
Here's Romeo's man. We found him in the churchyard.
FIRST WATCH
Hold him in safety till the Prince come hither.   183

    Enter Friar [Laurence], and another Watchman
    [with tools].

THIRD WATCH
Here is a friar, that trembles, sighs, and weeps.
We took this mattock and this spade from him
As he was coming from this churchyard's side.
FIRST WATCH
A great suspicion. Stay the Friar too.   187

    Enter the Prince [and attendants].

PRINCE
What misadventure is so early up
That calls our person from our morning rest?

    Enter Capels [Capulet and his Wife].

CAPULET
What should it be that is so shrieked abroad?
CAPULET'S WIFE
O, the people in the street cry "Romeo,"
Some "Juliet," and some "Paris," and all run
With open outcry toward our monument.
PRINCE
What fear is this which startles in our ears?   194
FIRST WATCH
Sovereign, here lies the County Paris slain,
And Romeo dead, and Juliet, dead before,
Warm and new killed.

---

180 ground basis (playing on the literal meaning in l. 179)
181 circumstance details   **183 in safety** under guard   **187 Stay** detain   **194 startles** cries alarmingly

PRINCE

Search, seek, and know how this foul murder comes.   198

FIRST WATCH

Here is a friar, and slaughtered Romeo's man,
With instruments upon them fit to open   200
These dead men's tombs.

CAPULET

O heavens! O wife, look how our daughter bleeds!
This dagger hath mista'en, for lo, his house   203
Is empty on the back of Montague,
And it mis-sheathèd in my daughter's bosom!

CAPULET'S WIFE

O me! This sight of death is as a bell
That warns my old age to a sepulcher.

Enter Montague.

PRINCE

Come, Montague, for thou art early up
To see thy son and heir now early down.

MONTAGUE

Alas, my liege, my wife is dead tonight;
Grief of my son's exile hath stopped her breath.
What further woe conspires against mine age?

PRINCE   Look, and thou shalt see.

MONTAGUE [*Seeing Romeo's body*]

O thou untaught! What manners is in this,   214
To press before thy father to a grave?   215

PRINCE

Seal up the mouth of outrage for a while,   216
Till we can clear these ambiguities
And know their spring, their head, their true descent;   218
And then will I be general of your woes   219
And lead you even to death. Meantime forbear,   220
And let mischance be slave to patience.   221
Bring forth the parties of suspicion.   222

---

198 know learn   **200 instruments** tools   **203 his house** its scabbard
214 untaught ill-mannered youth. (Said with affectionate irony.)   **215 press**
hasten, go   **216 outrage** outcry   **218 spring, head** source   **219 be . . . woes**
be leader in lamentation   **220 to death** i.e., (1) as far as the dead bodies
(2) so far in lamentation that we shall seem dead   **221 let . . . patience**
i.e., submit patiently to our misfortune   **222 of** under

FRIAR LAURENCE
  I am the greatest, able to do least,
  Yet most suspected, as the time and place
  Doth make against me, of this direful murder;   225
  And here I stand, both to impeach and purge   226
  Myself condemnèd and myself excused.   227
PRINCE
  Then say at once what thou dost know in this.
FRIAR LAURENCE
  I will be brief, for my short date of breath   229
  Is not so long as is a tedious tale.
  Romeo, there dead, was husband to that Juliet,
  And she, there dead, that Romeo's faithful wife.
  I married them, and their stol'n marriage day
  Was Tybalt's doomsday, whose untimely death
  Banished the new-made bridegroom from this city,
  For whom, and not for Tybalt, Juliet pined.
  You, to remove that siege of grief from her,
  Betrothed and would have married her perforce   238
  To County Paris. Then comes she to me,
  And with wild looks bid me devise some means
  To rid her from this second marriage,
  Or in my cell there would she kill herself.
  Then gave I her—so tutored by my art—
  A sleeping potion, which so took effect
  As I intended, for it wrought on her   245
  The form of death. Meantime I writ to Romeo   246
  That he should hither come as this dire night   247
  To help to take her from her borrowed grave,
  Being the time the potion's force should cease.
  But he which bore my letter, Friar John,
  Was stayed by accident, and yesternight   251
  Returned my letter back. Then all alone
  At the prefixèd hour of her waking
  Came I to take her from her kindred's vault,
  Meaning to keep her closely at my cell   255

225 make conspire, tell   **226–227 to . . . excused** to accuse myself of
what is to be condemned in me, and to exonerate myself where I ought
to be excused   **229 date of breath** time left to live   **238 perforce** by
compulsion   **245 wrought** fashioned   **246 form** appearance   **247 as
this** this very   **251 stayed** stopped   **255 closely** secretly

Till I conveniently could send to Romeo.
But when I came, some minute ere the time
Of her awakening, here untimely lay
The noble Paris and true Romeo dead.
She wakes, and I entreated her come forth
And bear this work of heaven with patience.
But then a noise did scare me from the tomb,
And she, too desperate, would not go with me,
But, as it seems, did violence on herself.
All this I know, and to the marriage
Her nurse is privy; and if aught in this   266
Miscarried by my fault, let my old life
Be sacrificed some hour before his time   268
Unto the rigor of severest law.

PRINCE
We still have known thee for a holy man.   270
Where's Romeo's man? What can he say to this?

BALTHASAR
I brought my master news of Juliet's death,
And then in post he came from Mantua   273
To this same place, to this same monument.
This letter he early bid me give his father,   275
                              [*Showing a letter*]
And threatened me with death, going in the vault,
If I departed not and left him there.

PRINCE [*Taking the letter*]
Give me the letter. I will look on it.
Where is the County's page, that raised the watch?
Sirrah, what made your master in this place?   280

PAGE
He came with flowers to strew his lady's grave,
And bid me stand aloof, and so I did.
Anon comes one with light to ope the tomb,
And by and by my master drew on him,
And then I ran away to call the watch.

PRINCE
This letter doth make good the Friar's words,
Their course of love, the tidings of her death;
And here he writes that he did buy a poison

266 **privy** in on the secret   268 **his** its   270 **still** always   273 **post**
haste   275 **early** early in the morning   280 **made** did

Of a poor 'pothecary, and therewithal   289
Came to this vault to die, and lie with Juliet.
Where be these enemies? Capulet, Montague,
See what a scourge is laid upon your hate,
That heaven finds means to kill your joys with love.   293
And I, for winking at your discords, too   294
Have lost a brace of kinsmen. All are punished.   295

CAPULET
O brother Montague, give me thy hand.
This is my daughter's jointure, for no more   297
Can I demand.

MONTAGUE   But I can give thee more,
For I will raise her statue in pure gold,   299
That whiles Verona by that name is known
There shall no figure at such rate be set   301
As that of true and faithful Juliet.

CAPULET
As rich shall Romeo's by his lady's lie;
Poor sacrifices of our enmity!

PRINCE
A glooming peace this morning with it brings;
   The sun, for sorrow, will not show his head.
Go hence to have more talk of these sad things.
   Some shall be pardoned, and some punishèd;
For never was a story of more woe
Than this of Juliet and her Romeo.   [*Exeunt.*]

---

289 therewithal i.e., with the poison   **293 kill your joys** (1) destroy your happiness (2) kill your children. **with** by means of   **294 winking at** shutting my eyes to   **295 a brace of** two   **297 jointure** marriage portion   **299 raise** (The Quarto 2 reading, *raie*, is defended by some editors in the sense of "array," make ready.)   **301 rate** value

Date and Text

A corrupt and unregistered quarto of *Romeo and Juliet* appeared in 1597 with the following title:

AN EXCELLENT conceited Tragedie OF Romeo and Iuliet, As it hath been often (with great applause) plaid publiquely, by the right Honourable the L. of *Hunsdon* his Seruants. LONDON, Printed by Iohn Danter. 1597.

This was a pirated edition issued by an unscrupulous publisher, no doubt to capitalize on the play's great popularity. It seems to have been memorially reconstructed by two or more actors (probably those playing Romeo and Paris), and possibly thereafter used as a promptbook. Its appearance seems to have caused the issuance two years later of a clearly authoritative version:

THE MOST EXCELLENT and lamentable Tragedie, of Romeo and *Iuliet. Newly corrected, augmented, and amended:* As it hath bene sundry times publiquely acted, by the right Honourable the Lord Chamberlaine his Seruants. LONDON Printed by Thomas Creede, for Cuthbert Burby, and are to be sold at his shop neare the Exchange. 1599.

This text is some 800 lines longer than the first, and corrects errors in that earlier version. It seems at one point, however, to have been contaminated by the first quarto, as though the manuscript source for the second quarto (probably the author's foul papers) was defective at some point. A passage from 1.2.53 to 1.3.34 was apparently set directly from the first quarto. (On this matter, see George W. Williams's old-spelling edition of the play, Duke Univ. Press, 1964). The first quarto may also have influenced the second quarto in some other isolated instances. Despite this contamination, however, the second quarto is the authoritative text except for the passage of direct indebtedness to the first quarto. The second quarto served as the basis for the third quarto (1609) which in turn served as copy for the fourth quarto (undated, but placed in 1622) and the First Folio of 1623. A fifth quarto appeared in 1637. The Folio text may embody a few authoritative readings of its own, perhaps by way of reference to a theatrical manuscript.

Francis Meres, in his *Palladis Tamia: Wit's Treasury* (a slender volume on contemporary literature and art; valuable because it lists most of the plays of Shakespeare that existed at that time), assigns the play to Shakespeare in 1598. So does John Weever in his *Epigrams* of 1599. Internal evidence on dating is not reliable. The Nurse observes that " 'Tis since the earthquake now eleven years" (1.3.24); but suitable earthquakes have been discovered in 1580, 1583, 1584, and 1585, giving us a wide choice of dates even if we accept the dubious proposition that the Nurse is speaking accurately. Astronomical reckoning of the position of the moon at the time the play purportedly takes place ("A fortnight and odd days" before Lammastide, August 1, 1.3.16) indicates the year 1596; again, however, we have no reason to assume Shakespeare cared about this sort of internal accuracy. More suggestive perhaps is the argument that Danter's unauthorized publication in 1597 was seeking to exploit a popular new play, one the acting company certainly did not yet wish to see published, since it was a money-maker. Danter assigns the play to Lord Hunsdon's servants, a name that Shakespeare's company could have used only from July 22, 1596 (when the old Lord Chamberlain, Henry Carey, first Lord Hunsdon, died) to April 17, 1597 (when George Carey, second Lord Hunsdon, was appointed to his father's erstwhile position as Lord Chamberlain). Danter could simply have been using the name of the company at the time he pirated the play, but he may also indicate performance in late 1596. Stylistically, the play is clearly of the "lyric" period of *A Midsummer Night's Dream* and *Richard II*. There are also stylistic affinities to the sonnets and to the narrative poems of 1593–1594. A date between 1594 and 1596 is likely, especially toward the latter end of this period. Whether the play comes before or after *A Midsummer Night's Dream* is, however, a matter of conjecture.

Textual Notes

These textual notes are not a historical collation, either of the early quartos and the early folios or of more recent editions; they are simply a record of departures in this edition from the copy text. The reading adopted in this edition appears in boldface, followed by the rejected reading from the copy text, i.e., the second quarto of 1599. Only major alterations in punctuation are noted. Changes in lineation are not indicated, nor are some minor and obvious typographical errors.

Abbreviations used:
Q1 the first quarto of 1597
Q2 the second quarto of 1599
s.d. stage direction
s.p. speech prefix

Copy text: the second quarto of 1599, except for 1.2.53–1.3.34, for which Q1 is the prior authority.

1.1. 27 it in [Q1] it **73 s.p. Citizens** Offi **76 s.p. Capulet's Wife** Wife
92 Verona's Neronas **120 drave** drive **147 his** is **153 sun** same
177 create [Q1] created **179 well-seeming** [Q1] welseeing **189 grief to** [Q1]
grief, too **192 lovers'** [Q1] loving **202 Bid a** [Q1] A **make** [Q1] makes
206 markman mark man **211 unharmed** [Q1] vncharmd **218 makes** make

1.2. 14 The earth Earth **32 on** one **38–39 written here** written. Here
46 One [Q1] on **70 and Livia** [Q1] Liuia [Q2] **79 thee** [Q1] you [Q2]
91 fires fier

1.3. 12 an [Q2] a [Q1] **18 shall** [Q1] stal [Q2] **33 wi' th'** [Q1: with] with the
[Q2] **50 s.p. [and elsewhere] Wife** Old La **66 disposition** [F] dispositions
67, 68 honor [Q1] houre **100 it fly** [Q1] flie **105 s.p. [and elsewhere] Wife**
Mo

1.4. 7–8 [Q1; not in Q2] **23 s.p. Mercutio** Horatio **39 done** [Q1] dum **42 Of**
Or **45 like lamps** [Q1] lights lights **47 five fine** **57 atomi** [Q1] ottamie
59–61 [these lines follow l. 69 in Q2] **66 film** Philome **69 maid** [Q1] man
72 O'er [Q1] On **74 on** one **76 breaths** [Q1] breath **80 parson's** Persons
81 dreams he [Q1] he dreams **90 elflocks** Elklocks **111 fofreit** [Q1] fofreit

1.5. s.d. [Q2 adds: "Enter Romeo"] **1 s.p. First Servingman** Ser [also at ll. 6
and 12] **3 s.p. Second Servingman** 1 **11 s.p. Third Servingman** 2
14 s.p. Fourth Servingman 3 **17 s.p. Capulet** 1. Capu [also at ll. 35 and 40]
18 a bout about **96 ready** [Q1] did readie

2.0 Chorus **1 s.p. Chorus** [not in Q2] **4 matched** match

2.1. 7 Nay . . . too [assigned in Q2 to Benvolio] **10 one** [Q1] on
11 Pronounce [Q1] prouaunt **dove** [Q1] day **13 heir** [Q1] her **14 trim** [Q1]
true **39 open-arse, and** open, or

2.2. 16 do [Q1] to **20 eyes** [Q1] eye **41–42 nor any . . . name** ô be some
other name / Belonging to a man **45 were** [Q1] wene **58 not yet** yet not
82 pilot Pylat **83 washed** [Q1] washeth **92–93 false . . . They** false at louers

periuries. / They **101 more coying** [Q1] coying **110 circled** [Q1] circle
149, 151 s.p. Nurse [not in Q2] **150, 151 s.p. Juliet** [not in Q2] **163 than
mine** then **170 years** [Q1] yeare **180 gyves** giues **187 Sleep . . . breast** [Q1;
assigned in Q2 to Juliet] **189–190** [preceded in Q2 by an earlier version of
ll. 1–4 of the next scene, in which "fleckled darkness" reads "darknesse
fleckted" and "and Titan's fiery wheels" reads "made by *Tytans* wheeles"]

2.3. 2 Check'ring [Q1] Checking **4 fiery** [Q1] burning **51 wounded. Both
our** wounded both, our **85 not. She whom** [Q1] me not, her

2.4. 18 s.p. Benvolio [Q1] Ro. **28–29 phantasimes** phantacies **33 pardon-
me's** pardons mees **40 but a** a **113–114 for himself** [Q1] himself
205 dog's dog **212 s.d. Exeunt** Exit

2.5. 5 glide glides **11 three** there **15 And M.** And **26 I had** [Q1] I

2.6. 18 gossamer gossamours **27 music's** musicke

3.1. 2 Capels are Capels **67 injured** iniuried **73 stoccata** stucatho **90 your
houses** houses **107 soundly too. Your** soundly, to your **121 Alive He gan**
123 fire-eyed [Q1] fier end **136, 138 s.p. First Citizen** Citti **165 agile** [Q1]
aged **183 s.p. Montague** Capu **191 I** [Q1] It **196 s.d. Exeunt** Exit

3.2. 1 s.p. Juliet [not in Q2] **9 By** And by **47 darting** arting **49 shut** shot
51 of my my **60 one** on **72 It . . . did** [assigned in Q2 to Juliet] **73 O . . .
face** [assigned in Q2 to Nurse] **76 Dove-feathered** Rauenous douefeatherd
79 damnèd dimme **143 s.d. Exeunt** Exit

3.3. s.d. [Q2 has "Enter Friar and Romeo"] **39** [Q2 follows with a line:
"This may flyes do, when I from this must flie"] **43** [printed in Q2 before
l. 40] **52 Thou** [Q1] Then **61 madmen** [Q1] mad man **70 s.d. Knock** Enter
Nurse, and knocke **73 s.d. Knock** They knocke **75 s.d. Knock** Slud knock
80 s.d. Enter Nurse [at l. 78 in Q2] **110 denote** [Q1] deuote **117 lives** [Q1]
lies **144 pouts upon** puts vp **168 disguised** disguise

3.4. 10 s.d. [and elsewhere] Wife La **13 be** me

3.5. 13 exhaled exhale **19 the** the the **31 changed** change **36 s.d. Enter
Nurse** Enter Madame and Nurse **54 s.p. Juliet** Ro **67 s.d.** [bracketed s.d.
from Q1] **82 pardon him** padon **130–131 body . . . a bark** body? / Thou
counterfeits. A bark **139 gives** giue **142 How? Will** How will
151–152 proud . . . Thank proud mistresse minion you? / Thanke
160 s.p. [and elsewhere] Capulet Fa **172 s.p. and text Capulet** O, God-i'-
good-e'en** Father, ò Godigeden **173 s.p. Nurse** [not in Q2] **182 liened** liand

4.1. 7 talked [Q1] talke **45 cure** [Q1] care **46 Ah** [Q1] O **72 slay** [Q1] stay
78 off [Q1] of **83 chopless** [Q1] chapels **85 his tomb** his **98 breath** [Q1]
breast **100 wanny** many **110 In** Is [Q2 follows with a line: "Be borne to
buriall in thy kindreds graue"] **111 shalt** shall **115 and he** an he
116 waking walking **126 s.d. Exeunt** Exit

4.2. 3, 6 s.p. Servingman Ser **14 willed** wield **38 s.p. [and elsewhere] Wife**
Mo **47 s.d. Exeunt** Exit

4.3. 49 wake walke

4.4. 1 s.p. [and elsewhere] Wife La **12 s.d. Exeunt** Exit **15 s.p. First Servingman** Fel **18 s.p. Second Servingman** Fel **21 Thou** Twou **faith** father
23 s.d. [at l. 21 in Q2]

4.5. 41 long [Q1] loue   **51 behold** bedold   **65 cure** care   **65–66 not . . .
Heaven** not, / In these confusions heauen   **82 fond** some   **96 s.p. First
Musician** Musi   **99, 103 s.p. First Musician** Fid   **99 by** [Q1] my. [Q2 has s.d.
here: "Exit omnes"]   **s.d. Enter Peter** Enter Will Kemp   **107 s.p. First
Musician** Minstrels [and subsequently in this scene indicated by *Minst* or
Minstrel]   **123 Then . . . wit** [assigned in Q2 to 2 M]   **127 And . . . oppress**
[Q1; not in Q2]   **133, 136 Pretty** [Q1] Prates   **145 s.d. Exeunt** Exit

5.1. 15 fares my [Q1] doth my Lady   **17, 27, 32 s.p. Balthasar** Man   **24 e'en**
in   **defy** [Q1] denie   **33 s.d.** [at l. 32 in Q2]   **76 pay** [Q1] pray

5.3. 3 yew [Q1] young   **21 s.d. [Balthasar]** [Q1] Peter   **40, 43 s.p. Balthasar**
Pet   **68 conjuration** commiration   **71 s.p. Page** Boy [Q1; s.p. missing in Q2
and line treated as a s.d.]   **102 fair** faire? I will beleeue   **107 palace** pallat
108 [Q2 has four undeleted lines here: "Depart againe, come lye thou in my
arme, / Heer's to thy health, where ere thou tumblest in. / O true Appotheca-
rie! / Thy drugs are quicke. Thus with a kisse I die."]   **123 s.p. [and else-
where] Balthasar** Man   **137 yew** yong   **168 s.p. First Watch** Watch [also at
ll. 172, 195, 199]   **171 s.p. Page** Watch boy   **182 s.p. Second Watch** Watch
183, 187 s.p. First Watch Chief. watch   **187 too** too too   **190 shrieked** shrike
194 our your   **199 slaughtered** Slaughter   **201** [Q2 has a s.d. here: "Enter
Capulet and his wife"]   **209 early** [Q1] earling   **232 that** thats
274–275 place . . . This place. To this same monument / This   **281 s.p. Page**
Boy   **299 raise** raie

Shakespeare's Sources

Shakespeare's chief source for *Romeo and Juliet* was a long narrative poem (a selection of which follows) by Arthur Brooke called *The Tragical History of Romeus and Juliet, written first in Italian by Bandell and now in English by Ar. Br.* (1562). Other English versions of this popular legend were available to Shakespeare, in particular in William Painter's *The Palace of Pleasure* (1566), but Shakespeare shows only a passing indebtedness to it. Brooke mentions having seen (prior to 1562) a play about the two lovers, but such an old play is not likely to have been of much service to Shakespeare. Nor does he appear to have extensively consulted the various continental versions that lay behind Brooke's poem. Still, these versions help explain the genesis of the story.

The use of a sleeping potion to escape an unwelcome marriage goes back at least to the *Ephesiaca* of Xenophon of Ephesus (by the fifth century A.D.). Masuccio of Salerno, in his *Il Novellino* (1476), seems to have been the first to combine this sleeping potion story with an ironic aftermath of misunderstanding and suicide (as found in the Pyramus and Thisbe story of Ovid's *Metamorphoses*). In Masuccio's account, the lovers Mariotto and Giannozza of Siena are secretly married by a friar. When Mariotto kills a prominent citizen of Siena in a quarrel, he is banished to Alexandria. Giannozza, to avoid marriage with a suitor of her father's choosing, takes a sleeping potion given her by the friar and is buried as though dead. She is thereupon taken from the tomb by the friar and sent on her way to Alexandria. Mariotto, however, having failed to hear from her because the messenger is intercepted by pirates, returns in disguise to her tomb where he is discovered and executed. Giannozza, hearing this sad news, retires to a Sienese convent and dies of a broken heart.

In Luigi da Porto's *Historia novellamente ritrovata di due Nobili Amanti* (published c. 1530), based on Masuccio's account, the scene shifts to Verona. Despite the feuding of their two families, the Montecchi and the Cappelletti, Romeo and Guilietta meet and fall in love at a carnival ball. Romeo at once forgets his unrequited passion for a scornful lady. Friar Lorenzo, an experimenter in magic, secretly marries the lovers. Romeo tries to avoid brawling with the Cappelletti, but when some of his own kinsmen suffer defeat, he kills Theobaldo Cappelletti. After Romeo's departure for Mantua, Guilietta's family arranges a match for her with the Count of Lodrone. Friar Lorenzo gives Guilietta a sleeping potion and sends a letter to Romeo by a fellow friar, but this messenger is unable to find Romeo in Mantua. Romeo, hearing of Guilietta's supposed death from her servant Peter, returns to Verona with a poison he already possesses. Guilietta awakens in time to converse with Romeo before he dies. Then, refusing the Friar's advice to retire to a convent, she dies by stopping her own breath. This story provides no equivalents for Mercutio and the Nurse, although a young man named Marcuccio appears briefly at the Cappelletti's ball.

Da Porto's version inspired that of Matteo Bandello in his *Novelle* of 1554. Some details are added: Romeo goes to the ball in a vizard (mask), he has a servant named Pietro, a rope ladder is given to the Nurse enabling Romeo to visit Julietta's chamber before their marriage, Romeo obtains a poison from one Spolentino, etc. The young man at the ball, Marcuccio, is now named Mercutio but is still a minor figure. This Bandello version was translated into French by Pierre Boaistuau in his *Histoires Tragiques* (1559); Boaistuau adds the Apothecary (who is racked and hanged for his part in the tragedy), and has Romeo die before Juliet awakens and slays herself with Romeo's dagger.

Despite Arthur Brooke's implication on the title page that his version is based on Bandello, the narrative poem *Romeus and Juliet* is taken from Boaistuau. As can be seen in the following selection, Brooke's is a severely pious work written in "Poulter's Measure," couplets with alternating lines of six and seven feet. Brooke openly disapproves of the lovers' carnality and haste, although fortunately the story itself remains sympathetic to Romeus and Juliet. Brooke stresses star-crossed fortune and the antithesis of love and hate. He reduces Juliet's age from eighteen (as in Bandello) to sixteen. (Shakespeare further reduced her age to less than fourteen.) Brooke's narrative is generally close to Shakespeare's, though with important exceptions. Shakespeare compresses time from some nine months to a few days. In

Brooke, for example, some two weeks elapse between the masked ball and Romeus's encounter with Juliet in her garden, and about two months elapse between the marriage and Tybalt's death. In Shakespeare, Capulet moves the wedding up from Thursday to Wednesday, thereby complicating the time schedule for the lovers. Shakespeare also unifies his play by such devices as introducing Tybalt and Paris early in the story; in Brooke, Tybalt appears only at the time he is slain, and Juliet's proposed marriage to Count Paris emerges as a threat only after Romeus's banishment. Shakespeare's greatest transformation is of the characters. Brooke's Juliet is scheming. His Mercutio remains a shadowy figure as in Bandello et al. Brooke's Nurse is unattractive, although she does occasionally hint at comic greatness: for example, she garrulously confides to Romeus the details of Juliet's infancy and then keeps Juliet on tenterhooks while she prates about Romeus's fine qualities (ll. 631–714). Even if Shakespeare's play is incomparably superior to Brooke's drably versified poem, the indebtedness is extensive.

The Tragical History of Romeus and Juliet
By Arthur Brooke

There is beyond the Alps a town of ancient fame
Whose bright renown yet shineth clear. Verona men it
    name,
Built in an happy time, built on a fertile soil,
Maintainèd by the heavenly fates and by the townish
    toil.
. . . .
There were two ancient stocks, which Fortune high
    did place
Above the rest, endued with wealth and nobler of
    their race,
Loved of the common sort, loved of the Prince alike—
And like unhappy were they both when Fortune list
    to strike—   28
Whose praise with equal blast Fame in her trumpet
    blew.
The one was clepèd Capilet and th'other Montague.   30
  A wonted use it is that men of likely sort—   31
I wot not by what fury forced—envy each others'
    port.   32
So these, whose equal state bred envy pale of hue;
And then of grudging envy's root, black hate and
    rancor grew.
As of a little spark oft riseth mighty fire,
So, of a kindled spark of grudge, in flames flash out
    their ire.   36
And then their deadly food, first hatched of trifling
    strife,
Did bathe in blood of smarting wounds; it reavèd
    breath and life.   38
No legend lie I tell; scarce yet their eyes be dry   39
That did behold this grisly sight with wet and
    weeping eye.

---

28 like alike. **list** pleased **30 clepèd** named **31 wonted use** customary behavior. **likely sort** equal rank **32 wot** know. **port** style of living **36 grudge** resentment **38 reavèd** robbed, took away **39 legend** unauthentic

But when the prudent Prince who there the scepter
   held
So great a new disorder in his commonweal beheld,
By gentle means he sought their choler to assuage   43
And by persuasion to appease their blameful furious
   rage.
But both his words and time the Prince hath spent in
   vain;
So rooted was the inward hate, he lost his busy pain.
When friendly sage advice ne gentle words avail,   47
By thundering threats and princely power their
   courage gan he quail,   48
In hope that when he had the wasting flame
   suppressed,
In time he should quite quench the sparks that
   burned within their breast.
   Now whilst these kindreds do remain in this estate
And each with outward friendly show doth hide his
   inward hate,
One Romeus, who was of race a Montague,
Upon whose tender chin as yet no manlike beard
   there grew,
Whose beauty and whose shape so far the rest did
   stain   55
That from the chief of Veron youth he greatest fame
   did gain,
Hath found a maid so fair (he found so foul his hap),   57
Whose beauty, shape, and comely grace did so his
   heart entrap
That from his own affairs his thought she did
   remove.
Only he sought to honor her, to serve her, and to love.   60
To her he writeth oft; oft messengers are sent.
At length, in hope of better speed, himself the lover
   went   62
Present to plead for grace which, absent, was not
   found,   63
And to discover to her eye his new-receivèd wound.   64

43 choler anger **47 ne** nor **48 gan he quail** he tried to end, suppress
55 stain eclipse **57 so foul his hap** so miserable his fortune **60 Only
he** he only **62 speed** success **63 Present** in person, or presently
64 discover reveal, present

But she, that from her youth was fostered evermore
With virtue's food and taught in school of wisdom's
    skillful lore,
By answer did cut off th' affections of his love,
That he no more occasion had so vain a suit to move. 68

[After many months of this hopeless wooing, Romeus is
ready to leave Verona, but is instead persuaded by a friend
to cure his lovesickness by finding some other place to bestow his "witless wandering heart." Romeus agrees to fre-
quent every place where ladies are accustomed to gather.]

   The weary winter nights restore the Christmas
       games,
And now the season doth invite to banquet townish
    dames.
And first, in Capel's house, the chief of all the kin
Spar'th for no cost the wonted use of banquets to
    begin.
No lady fair or foul was in Verona town,
No knight or gentleman of high or low renown
But Capilet himself hath bid unto his feast,
Or, by his name in paper sent, appointed as a guest.
Young damsels thither flock, of bachelors a rout,   163
Not so much for the banquet's sake as beauties to
    search out.
But not a Montague would enter at his gate—
For, as you heard, the Capilets and they were at
    debate—
Save Romeus; and he, in mask with hidden face,
The supper done, with other five did press into the
    place.
When they had masked awhile with dames in courtly
    wise,
All did unmask. The rest did show them to their
    ladies' eyes,
But bashful Romeus with shamefast face forsook
The open press, and him withdrew into the
    chamber's nook.   172

68 vain hopeless

163 rout large assemblage   **172 press** crowd.   **him** himself

But brighter than the sun the waxen torches shone,
That, maugre what he could, he was espied of
    everyone,   174
But of the women chief, their gazing eyes that threw
To wonder at his sightly shape and beauty's spotless
    hew
With which the heavens him had and nature so
    bedecked
That ladies thought the fairest dames were foul in his
    respect.
And in their head besides another wonder rose:
How he durst put himself in throng among so many
    foes.
Of courage stout they thought his coming to
    proceed—
And women love an hardy heart, as I in stories read.
  The Capilets disdain the presence of their foe,
Yet they suppress their stirrèd ire—the cause I do not
    know.
Perhaps t' offend their guests the courteous knights
    are loath.
Perhaps they stay from sharp revenge, dreading the
    Prince's wroth.   186
Perhaps for that they shamed to exercise their rage
Within their house 'gainst one alone, and him of
    tender age.
They use no taunting talk, ne harm him by their deed;
They neither say "What mak'st thou here?" ne yet
    they say "God speed."
So that he freely might the ladies view at ease,
And they also, beholding him, their change of fancies
    please;
Which nature had him taught to do with such a grace
That there was none but joyèd at his being there in
    place.
With upright beam he weighed the beauty of each
    dame,   195
And judged who best, and who next her, was wrought
    in nature's frame.

174 maugre in spite of **186 stay** abstain. **wroth** wrath **195 upright beam** i.e., the scales of judgment

At length he saw a maid right fair, of perfect shape,
Which Theseus or Paris would have chosen to their
    rape.   198
Whom erst he never saw, of all she pleased him most. 199
Within himself he said to her, "Thou justly mayst
    thee boast
Of perfect shape's renown and beauty's sounding
    praise,
Whose like ne hath ne shall be seen, ne liveth in our
    days!"   202
And whilst he fixed on her his partial piercèd eye,   203
His former love, for which of late he ready was to
    die,
Is now as quite forgot as it had never been.
The proverb saith, "Unminded oft are they that are
    unseen."   206
And as out of a plank a nail a nail doth drive,
So novel love out of the mind the ancient love doth
    rive.   208
This sudden-kindled fire in time is wox so great   209
That only death and both their bloods might quench
    the fiery heat.
  When Romeus saw himself in this new tempest
    tossed,
Where both was hope of pleasant sport and danger to
    be lost,
He, doubtful, scarcely knew what countenance to
    keep.   213
In Lethe's flood his wonted flames were quenched
    and drenchèd deep.   214
Yea, he forgets himself, ne is the wretch so bold
To ask her name that without force hath him in
    bondage fold.   216

---

198 to their rape for seizing and carrying off   **199 Whom . . . saw** she
whom he had never seen before   **202 ne hath ne shall be** has never been
and never will be   **203 partial piercèd** favorably disposed and pierced
(by her beauty)   **206 Unminded . . . unseen** out of sight, out of mind
208 novel new.   **ancient** former, old.   **rive** pull, tear   **209 wox** waxed,
grown   **213 doubtful** full of doubts and fears   **214 Lethe's flood** the
river of forgetfulness.   **wonted** accustomed, former.   **drenchèd**
drowned   **216 fold** enfolded, confined

Ne how t' unloose his bonds doth the poor fool
    devise,
But only seeketh by her sight to feed his hungry eyes.
Through them he swalloweth down love's sweet
    empoisoned bait.
How surely are the wareless rapt by those that lie in
    wait?   220
So is the poison spread throughout his bones and
    veins
That in a while—alas the while!—it hasteth deadly
    pains.
    Whilst Juliet—for so this gentle damsel hight—   223
From side to side on everyone did cast about her
    sight.
At last her floating eyes were anchored fast on him
Who for her sake did banish health and freedom from
    each limb.
He in her sight did seem to pass the rest as far
As Phoebus' shining beams do pass the brightness of
    a star.
In wait lay warlike Love with golden bow and shaft,   229
And to his ear with steady hand the bowstring up he
    raft.   230
Till now she had escaped his sharp inflaming dart;
Till now he listed not assault her young and tender
    heart.   232
His whetted arrow, loosed, so touched her to the
    quick
That through the eye it strake the heart, and there the
    head did stick.
It booted not to strive, forwhy she wanted strength;   235
The weaker aye unto the strong of force must yield at
    length.   236
The pomps now of the feast her heart gins to despise,
And only joyeth when her eyen meet with her lover's
    eyes.

---

220 wareless unwary.   **rapt** seized   **223 Whilst** meanwhile.   **hight** was
named   **229 Love** Cupid   **230 raft** pulled   **232 he listed not** he (Cupid)
chose not to   **235 booted** availed.   **forwhy** because.   **wanted** was
lacking in   **236 aye** ever, always.   **of force** necessarily

When their new-smitten hearts had fed on loving
   gleams,
Whilst passing to and fro their eyes ymingled were
   their beams,   240
Each of these lovers gan by other's looks to know
That friendship in their breast had root, and both
   would have it grow.
  When thus in both their hearts had Cupid made his
   breach,
And each of them had sought the mean to end the
   war by speech,   244
Dame Fortune did assent their purpose to advance:
With torch in hand, a comely knight did fetch her
   forth to dance.
She quit herself so well, and with so trim a grace,   247
That she the chief praise wan that night from all
   Verona race;   248
The whilst our Romeus a place had warily won   249
Nigh to the seat where she must sit, the dance once
   being done.
  Fair Juliet turnèd to her chair with pleasant cheer, 251
And glad she was her Romeus approachèd was so
   near.
At th' one side of her chair, her lover Romeo;
And on the other side there sat one called Mercutio,
A courtier that eachwhere was highly had in price, 255
For he was courteous of his speech and pleasant of
   device.
Even as a lion would among the lambs be bold,
Such was, among the bashful maids, Mercutio to
   behold.
With friendly grip he seized fair Juliet's snowish
   hand.
A gift he had, that nature gave him in his swaddling
   band,   260
That frozen mountain ice was never half so cold

---

240 their eyes . . . beams their eyebeams intertwined **244 mean** means
247 quit acquitted **248 wan** won **249 The whilst** meanwhile. **warily**
discreetly **251 turnèd** returned. **cheer** countenance **255 eachwhere**
everywhere. **highly . . . price** highly regarded **260 in . . . band** i.e., in
his cradle, from birth

As were his hands, though ne'er so near the fire he
   did them hold.
As soon as had the knight the virgin's right hand
   raught,   263
Within his trembling hand her left hath loving
   Romeus caught;
For he wist well himself for her abode most pain,   265
And well he wist she loved him best, unless she list to
   feign.   266
  Then she with tender hand his tender palm hath
   pressed.
What joy trow you was grafted so in Romeus' cloven
   breast?   268
The sudden sweet delight hath stoppèd quite his
   tongue,
Ne can he claim of her his right, ne crave redress of
   wrong.   270
But she espied straightway, by changing of his hue
From pale to red, from red to pale, and so from pale
   anew,
That vehement love was cause why so his tongue did
   stay,   273
And so much more she longed to hear what love
   could teach him say.
  When she had longèd long, and he long held his
   peace,
And her desire of hearing him by silence did
   increase,
At last, with trembling voice and shamefast cheer, the
   maid   277
Unto her Romeus turned herself and thus to him she
   said:
"O, blessèd be the time of thy arrival here!"
But, ere she could speak forth the rest, to her Love
   drew so near   280

---

263 raught grasped **265 For ... pain** i.e., for Romeus well knew that he
suffered more than anyone out of lovesickness for Juliet **266 she list to
feign** she was feigning **268 trow you** do you think **270 Ne ... wrong**
i.e., he can neither claim his right of love in her nor beg redress for the
injuries he suffers in love. (A legal metaphor.) **273 stay** cease, remain
silent **277 shamefast cheer** bashful countenance **280 Love** Cupid

And so within her mouth her tongue he gluèd fast   281
That not one word could scape her more than what
    already passed.
In great contented ease the young man straight is
    wrapped.
"What chance," quoth he, "unware to me, O lady
    mine, is happed,
That gives you worthy cause my coming here to
    bliss?"   285
Fair Juliet was come again unto herself by this.
First ruthfully she looked, then said, with smiling
    cheer,   287
"Marvel no whit, my heart's delight, my only knight
    and fere.   288
Mercutio's icy hand had all to-frozen mine,   289
And of thy goodness thou again hast warmèd it with
    thine."
Whereto with staid brow gan Romeus to reply: 291
"If so the gods have granted me such favor from the
    sky
That by my being here some service I have done
That pleaseth you, I am as glad as I a realm had won.   294
O well-bestowèd time, that hath the happy hire,   295
Which I would wish if I might have my wishèd
    heart's desire!
For I of God would crave, as price of pains forepast,   297
To serve, obey, and honor you, so long as life shall
    last—
As proof shall teach you plain, if that you like to try
His faultless truth that nill for aught unto his lady
    lie.   300
But if my touchèd hand have warmèd yours
    somedeal,   301
Assure yourself the heat is cold which in your hand
    you feel
Compared to such quick sparks and glowing furious
    gleed   303

281 he i.e., Cupid   **285 bliss** bless, give thanks for   **287 ruthfully** com-
passionately   **288 fere** mate, companion   **289 to-frozen** completely
frozen   **291 staid** fixed, set   **294 as I** as if I   **295 hire** recompense,
reward   **297 forepast** past   **300 truth** troth, faith.   **nill** will not
301 somedeal somewhat   **303 gleed** fire, ember

As from your beauty's pleasant eyne Love caused to
    proceed!   304

Which have so set on fire each feeling part of mine

That, lo, my mind doth melt away; my outward parts
    do pine,

And, but you help, all whole to ashes shall I turn.   307

Wherefore, alas! have ruth on him whom you do
    force to burn."   308

  Even with his ended tale the torches' dance had
    end,

And Juliet of force must part from her new-chosen
    friend.   310

His hand she claspèd hard, and all her parts did
    shake,

When, leisureless, with whispering voice thus did she
    answer make: 312

"You are no more your own, dear friend, than I am
    yours—

My honor saved—prest t' obey your will while life
    endures."   314

  Lo, here the lucky lot that seld true lovers find.   315

Each takes away the other's heart and leaves the own
    behind.   316

A happy life is love, if God grant from above

That heart with heart by even weight do make
    exchange of love.

  But Romeus, gone from her, his heart for care is
    cold.

He hath forgot to ask her name that hath his heart in
    hold!

With forgèd careless cheer, of one he seeks to know   321

Both how she hight and whence she came, that him
    enchanted so.   322

So hath he learned her name, and knoweth she is no
    guest;

Her father was a Capilet and master of the feast!

---

304 eyne eyes   **307 but** unless.   **all whole** wholly   **308 ruth** pity
310 of force of necessity   **312 leisureless** i.e., in haste   **314 My honor
saved** so long as my chastity is not violated.   **prest** ready, eager
315 seld seldom   **316 the own** i.e., his or her own   **321 forgèd careless
cheer** a look of pretended nonchalance   **322 hight** was named

Thus hath his foe in choice to give him life or death,   325
That scarcely can his woeful breast keep in the lively
     breath.
Wherefore with piteous plaint fierce Fortune doth he
     blame,
That in his ruth and wretched plight doth seek her
     laughing game.   328
And he reproveth Love, chief cause of his unrest,
Who ease and freedom hath exiled out of his youthful
     breast.
Twice hath he made him serve, hopeless of his
     reward.   331
Of both the ills, to choose the less I ween the choice
     were hard.   332
First to a ruthless one he made him sue for grace,
And now with spur he forceth him to run an endless
     race.
Amid these stormy seas one anchor doth him hold:
He serveth not a cruel one, as he had done of old,
And therefore is content, and chooseth still to serve,
Though hap should swear that guerdonless the
     wretched wight should starve.   338
The lot of Tantalus is, Romeus, like to thine:
For want of food amid his food the miser still doth
     pine.
  As careful was the maid what way were best devise
To learn his name that entertained her in so gentle
     wise,
Of whom her heart received so deep, so wide a
     wound.
An ancient dame she called to her and in her ear gan
     round.   344
This old dame in her youth had nursed her with her
     milk,
With slender needle taught her sew, and how to spin
     with silk.

325 in choice i.e., in her power   **328 doth seek . . . game** plays to amuse
herself   **331 hath . . . serve** i.e., has Cupid made Romeo obey the god of
love   **332 ween** think, suppose   **338 Though . . . starve** i.e., even though
Fate should swear an oath that the wretched Romeo must perish without reward   **344 round** whisper

"What twain are those," quoth she, "which press
    unto the door,
Whose pages in their hands do bear two torches light
    before?" 348
And then, as each of them had of his household
    name, 349
So she him named yet once again, the young and wily
    dame. 350
"And tell me who is he, with visor in his hand,
That yonder doth in masking weed beside the
    window stand?" 352
"His name is Romeus," said she, "a Montague,
Whose father's pride first stirred the strife which
    both your households rue."
  The word of "Montague" her joys did overthrow,
And straight, instead of happy hope, despair began to
    grow. 356
"What hap have I," quoth she, "to love my father's
    foe?
What, am I weary of my weal? What, do I wish my
    woe?" 358
But though her grievous pains distrained her tender
    heart, 359
Yet with an outward show of joy she cloakèd inward
    smart,
And of the courtlike dames her leave so courtly took
That none did guess the sudden change by changing
    of her look.

[Unable to sleep, Juliet ponders her predicament, "ycaught
in subtle snare," and wonders if, like Dido, she is being deceived by her lover's attractive outside. She decides in Romeus's favor, since, as Brooke editorializes, we can
persuade ourselves "to what we like" when the mind is cap-
tured by the fancy of love. Romeus meanwhile is likewise
driven "to forsake his weary bed" by restless thoughts.
Walking by Juliet's house, he catches a glimpse of her and

---

348 light lighted   **349 had . . . name** was named according to his family   **350 she . . . again** Juliet repeated each name aloud   **352 weed**
garments   **356 straight** at once   **358 weal** well-being   **359 distrained**
afflicted

soon discovers a garden plot that faces on her window, but,
fearful of detection by her kinsmen, he is unable to speak
with her for a week or two. Juliet meanwhile has been distracted by worry. At last they are able to converse in the
secrecy of night.]

Now, whilst with bitter tears her eyes as fountains
    run,
With whispering voice ybroke with sobs thus is her
    tale begun:
"O Romeus, of your life too lavish sure you are
That in this place and at this time to hazard it you
    dare!
What if your deadly foes, my kinsmen, saw you here?
Like lions wild your tender parts asunder would they
    tear.
In ruth and in disdain I, weary of my life,
With cruel hand by mourning heart would pierce
    with bloody knife.
For you, mine own, once dead, what joy should I have
    here?
And eke my honor stained, which I than life do hold
    more dear."   498
  "Fair lady mine, dame Juliet, my life," quod he,   499
"Even from my birth committed was to fatal sisters
    three.   500
They may, in spite of foes, draw forth my lively
    thread,   501
And they also—whoso saith nay—asunder may it
    shred.   502
But who to reave my life his rage and force would
    bend   503
Perhaps should try unto his pain how I it could
    defend.   504
Ne yet I love it so but always for your sake   505

---

498 **eke** also   499–500 **my life . . . three** i.e., from the time of my birth
my life has been in the hands of the three Fates (Clotho, Lachesis, and
Atropos)   501 **draw forth** extend, lengthen   502 **whoso saith nay** no
matter who wishes to deny it   503 **who to reave** whoever to bereave me
of. **bend** aim, intend   504 **unto his pain** to his cost   505 **it** i.e., life

A sacrifice to death I would my wounded corpse
    betake.   506
If my mishap were such that here, before your sight,
I should restore again to death of life my borrowed
    light,   508
This one thing and no more my parting sprite would
    rue: 509
That part he should before that you by certain trial
    knew   510
The love I owe to you, the thrall I languish in,   511
And how I dread to lose the gain which I do hope to
    win,
And how I wish for life, not for my proper ease,   513
But that in it you might I love, you honor, serve, and
    please   514
Till deadly pangs the sprite out of the corpse shall
    send."
And thereupon he sware an oath, and so his tale had
    end.
  Now love and pity boil in Juliet's ruthful breast.
In window on her leaning arm her weary head doth
    rest,
Her bosom bathed in tears to witness inward pain.
With dreary cheer to Romeus thus answered she
    again:
  "Ah, my dear Romeus, keep in these words!" quod
    she.   521
"For lo, the thought of such mischance already
    maketh me
For pity and for dread wellnigh to yield up breath.
In even balance peisèd are my life and eke my death,   524
For so my heart is knit, yea, made one self with yours
That sure there is no grief so small by which your
    mind endures
But, as you suffer pain, so I do bear in part—

---

506 A . . . betake I would deliver over my wounded body to death as a
sacrifice (for your sake)   **508 I . . . light** i.e., I should give back to death
the borrowed light of my life   **509 sprite** spirit, soul   **510 That . . . that**
i.e., that my soul should depart before   **511 thrall** thralldom, bondage
513 proper own   **514 you might I love** I might love you   **521 keep in** do
not utter   **524 peisèd** weighed.   **eke** also

Although it lessens not your grief—the half of all
　　your smart.
But these things overpast, if of your health and mine
You have respect, or pity aught my teary weeping
　　eyen,　　　　　　　　　　　　　　　　　　　　530
In few unfeignèd words your hidden mind unfold,
That, as I see your pleasant face your heart I may
　　behold.
For if you do intend my honor to defile,
In error shall you wander still, as you have done this
　　while.
But if your thought be chaste and have on virtue
　　ground,
If wedlock be the end and mark which your desire
　　hath found,
Obedience set aside unto my parents due,　　　537
The quarrel eke that long ago between our
　　households grew,　　　　　　　　　　　　538
Both me and mine I will all whole to you betake　539
And, following you whereso you go, my father's
　　house forsake.
But if by wanton love and by unlawful suit
You think in ripest years to pluck my maidenhood's
　　dainty fruit,　　　　　　　　　　　　　　542
You are beguiled, and now your Juliet you beseeks　543
To cease your suit and suffer her to live among her
　　likes."　　　　　　　　　　　　　　　　544
　　Then Romeus, whose thought was free from foul
　　desire,
And to the top of virtue's height did worthily aspire,
Was filled with greater joy than can my pen
　　express—
Or, till they have enjoyed the like, the hearer's heart
　　can guess.
And then with joinèd hands heaved up into the skies,

---

530 teary tear-filled. **eyen** eyes **537–538 Obedience . . . grew** setting aside the obedience due my parents and also the allegiances of the ancient quarrel between our two families **539 all whole** wholly. **betake** give **542 ripest years** i.e., the years when beauty is most in flower **543 you beseeks** beseeches you **544 likes** equals, i.e., family and friends

He thanks the gods, and from the heavens for
    vengeance down he cries
If he have other thought but as his lady spake.
And then his look he turned to her and thus did
    answer make:
  "Since, lady, that you like to honor me so much
As to accept me for your spouse, I yield myself for
    such.
In true witness whereof, because I must depart,
Till that my deed do prove my word, I leave in pawn
    my heart.
Tomorrow eke betimes, before the sun arise,   557
To Friar Laurence will I wend, to learn his sage
    advice.
He is my ghostly sire, and oft he hath me taught   559
What I should do in things of weight when I his aid
    have sought.
And at this selfsame hour, I plight you here my faith,   561
I will be here, if you think good, and tell you what he
    saith."
She was contented well, else favor found he none   563
That night, at Lady Juliet's hand, save pleasant words
    alone.
  This barefoot friar girt with cord his grayish weed,
For he of Francis' order was, a friar, as I rede.   566
Not as the most was he, a gross unlearned fool,   567
But doctor of divinity proceeded he in school.   568
The secrets eke he knew in nature's works that lurk;   569
By magic's art most men supposed that he could
    wonders work.
Ne doth it ill beseem divines those skills to know
If on no harmful deed they do such skillfulness
    bestow.
For justly of no art can men condemn the use;
But right and reason's lore cry out against the lewd
    abuse.   574

---

557 betimes early   **559 ghostly** spiritual   **561 plight** pledge   **563 else**
otherwise   **566 rede** advise (or possibly *read*)   **567 Not . . . fool** he was
not, like most of his kind, a grossly unlearned fool   **568 proceeded**
advanced to the higher degree of   **569 eke** also   **574 lewd** wicked

The bounty of the Friar and wisdom hath so won
The townsfolks' hearts that wellnigh all to Friar
    Laurence run
To shrive themself—the old, the young, the great and
    small.   577
Of all he is belovèd well and honored much of all.
And, for he did the rest in wisdom far exceed,   579
The Prince by him, his counsel craved, was holp at
    time of need.   580
Betwixt the Capilets and him great friendship grew;
A secret and assurèd friend unto the Montague.
Loved of this young man more than any other guest,
The Friar eke of Verone youth aye likèd Romeus best,
For whom he ever hath, in time of his distress,
As erst you heard, by skillful lore found out his
    harm's redress.
  To him is Romeus gone, ne stayeth he till the
    morrow.
To him he painteth all his case: his passèd joy and
    sorrow,
How he hath her espied with other dames in dance,
And how that first to talk with her himself he did
    advance.
Their talk and change of looks he gan to him declare,
And how so fast by faith and troth they both
    ycoupled are,   592
That neither hope of life nor dread of cruel death
Shall make him false his faith to her while life shall
    lend him breath.   594
And then with weeping eyes he prays his ghostly sire
To further and accomplish all their honest heart's
    desire.
  A thousand doubts and more in th' old man's head
    arose;
A thousand dangers like to come the old man doth
    disclose.   598
And from the spousal rites he redeth him refrain;   599

577 shrive themself make their confessions **579 for** because **580 his**
counsel craved the Friar's advice being sought. **holp** helped **592 fast**
firmly **594 false** falsify **598 like** likely **599 redeth** advises

Perhaps he shall be bet advised within a week or
   twain.   600
  Advice is banished quite from those that follow
   love,
Except advice to what they like their bending mind
   do move.
As well the father might have counseled him to stay   603
That from a mountain's top thrown down is falling
   half the way   604
As warn his friend to stop, amid his race begun,
Whom Cupid with his smarting whip enforceth forth
   to run.   606
Part won by earnest suit, the Friar doth grant at last,
And part because he thinks the storms so lately
   overpast
Of both the households' wrath this marriage might
   appease,
So that they should not rage again, but quite forever
   cease.
The respite of a day he asketh to devise
What way were best, unknown, to end so great an
   enterprise.   612
The wounded man, that now doth deadly pains
   endure,   613
Scarce patient tarryeth whilst his leech doth make
   the salve to cure;   614
So Romeus hardly grants a short day and a night.   615
Yet needs he must, else must he want his only heart's
   delight.   616
  You see that Romeus no time or pain doth spare;
Think that the whilst fair Juliet is not devoid of care!   618
Young Romeus poureth forth his hap and his mishap
Into the Friar's breast, but where shall Juliet unwrap
The secrets of her heart? To whom shall she unfold
Her hidden burning love and eke her thought and
   cares so cold?

600 he . . . advised he will think better of it, be better advised
603 father i.e., friar   **603–604 stay That** stop an object that   **606 Whom**
him whom   **612 end** accomplish   **613 The wounded man** i.e., one who,
like Romeus, is wounded with love's arrow   **614 Scarce** scarcely.   **leech**
doctor (i.e., the Friar)   **615 hardly grants** reluctantly agrees to a delay
of   **616 want** lack   **618 the whilst** meanwhile

The Nurse, of whom I spake, within the chamber
   lay.
Upon the maid she waiteth still. To her she doth
   bewray   624
Her new-receivèd wound, and then her aid doth
   crave.
In her she saith it lies to spill, in her her life to save.   626
Not easily she made the froward Nurse to bow,   627
But, won at length, with promised hire she made a
   solemn vow   628
To do what she commands, as handmaid of her hest.   629
Her mistress' secrets hide she will within her covert
   breast.
   To Romeus she goes. Of him she doth desire
To know the mean of marriage, by counsel of the
   Friar.   632
"On Saturday," quod he, "if Juliet come to shrift,   633
She shall be shrived and married. How like you,
   Nurse, this drift?"   634
"Now, by my truth," quod she, "God's blessing have
   your heart!
For yet in all my life I have not heard of such a part.   636
Lord, how you young men can such crafty wiles
   devise,
If that you love the daughter well, to blear the
   mother's eyes!
An easy thing it is with cloak of holiness
To mock the silly mother that suspecteth nothing
   less.   640
But that it pleasèd you tell me of the case,   641
For all my many years, perhaps, I should have found
   it scarce.   642
Now, for the rest, let me and Juliet alone.
To get her leave, some feat excuse I will devise anon,   644

624 **still** always. **bewray** reveal   626 **spill** kill, destroy   627 **froward**
perverse, refractory. **bow** yield   628 **hire** monetary reward   629 **hest**
command   632 **mean** means   633 **shrift** confession   634 **She . . . shrived**
her confession will be heard   636 **part** thing   640 **silly** innocent, unsus-
pecting.   **nothing less** i.e., nothing at all   641 **But that** were it not that
642 **found it scarce** i.e., scarcely believed it   644 **feat** suitable

For that her golden locks by sloth have been
    unkempt,   645
Or for unwares some wanton dream the youthful
    damsel dreamt,
Or for in thoughts of love her idle time she spent,
Or otherwise within her heart deservèd to be shent.   648
I know her mother will in no case say her nay;
I warrant you she shall not fail to come on
    Saturday."
  And then she swears to him the mother loves her
    well;
And how she gave her suck in youth she leaveth not
    to tell.   652
"A pretty babe," quod she, "it was when it was
    young.
Lord, how it could full prettily have prated with it
    tongue!   654
A thousand times and more I laid her on my lap,
And clapped her on the buttock soft and kissed
    where I did clap.
And gladder then was I of such a kiss, forsooth,
Than I had been to have a kiss of some old lecher's
    mouth."
  And thus of Juliet's youth began this prating nurse,
And of her present state to make a tedious long
    discourse.
For, though he pleasure took in hearing of his love,
The message answer seemèd him to be of more
    behoof.   662
But when these beldams sit at ease upon their tail,   663
The day and eke the candlelight before their talk
    shall fail.
And part they say is true, and part they do devise;
Yet boldly do they chat of both when no man checks
    their lies.   666
  Then he six crowns of gold out of his pocket drew

---

645 For . . . unkempt i.e., that her hair is uncombed. (This is one of the excuses that the Nurse will use to cover Juliet's absence.) **648 shent** blamed **652 leaveth not** does not omit **654 it** its **662 behoof** benefit **663 beldams** old women **666 no man** no one

And gave them her. "A slight reward," quod he, "and
    so, adieu."
In seven years twice told she had not bowed so low   669
Her crooked knees as now they bow. She swears she
    will bestow
Her crafty wit, her time, and all her busy pain
To help him to his hopèd bliss, and, cowering down
    again,
She takes her leave and home she hies with speedy
    pace.
  The chamber door she shuts, and then she saith,
    with smiling face,
"Good news for thee, my girl, good tidings I thee
    bring!
Leave off thy wonted song of care, and now of
    pleasure sing.
For thou mayst hold thyself the happiest under sun,
That in so little while so well so worthy a knight hast
    won.
The best yshaped is he and hath the fairest face
Of all this town, and there is none hath half so good a
    grace,
So gentle of his speech, and of his counsel wise."
And still with many praises more she heaved him to
    the skies.   682
  "Tell me else what," quod she. "This evermore I
    thought.   683
But of our marriage, say at once, what answer have
    you brought?"
"Nay, soft," quoth she, "I fear your hurt by sudden
    joy."
"I list not play," quoth Juliet, "although thou list to
    toy."   686
How glad, trow you, was she when she had heard her
    say
No farther off than Saturday deferrèd was the day!
Again the ancient nurse doth speak of Romeus.

---

669 told counted   **682 still . . . skies** i.e., she continually praised him to
the skies   **683 Tell . . . thought** i.e., tell me something new, said Juliet; I
knew all this before. (Compare *Romeo and Juliet*, 2.5.46.)   **686 I list not
play** i.e., I'm not in a mood for jesting.   **toy** trifle

"And then," said she, "he spake to me, and then I
    spake him thus."
Nothing was done or said that she hath left untold
Save only one, that she forgot the taking of the gold.   692
    "There is no loss," quod she, "sweet wench, to loss
    of time,   693
Ne in thine age shalt thou repent so much of any
    crime.   694
For when I call to mind my former passèd youth,
One thing there is which most of all doth cause my
    endless ruth.   696
At sixteen years I first did choose my loving fere,   697
And I was fully ripe before, I dare well say, a year.   698
The pleasure that I lost that year so overpast
A thousand times I have bewept, and shall while life
    doth last.
In faith, it were a shame, yea, sin it were, iwis,   701
When thou mayst live in happy joy to set light by thy
    bliss."   702
She that this morning could her mistress' mind
    dissuade   703
Is now become an oratoress her lady to persuade.

[The "wily" Juliet gets permission to go with the Nurse to
shrift at Friar Lawrence's cell, where she and Romeus are
married. The Nurse provides a ladder of cords by which Romeus climbs to her window and consummates his marriage
to Juliet. Shortly after, the feud between the Capilets and
Montagues flares up again, and Tybalt, Juliet's cousin (mentioned now for the first time), challenges Romeus in the
streets, attacking so relentlessly that Romeus is forced to
lay aside his scruples and his secret loyalty to Juliet. Mercutio and Benvolio take no part in this scene. Romeus's banishment follows as a consequence of his killing Tybalt, and
the story proceeds much as in Shakespeare except that the
proposed marriage to Paris is not mentioned until after
Romeus's exile. When Romeus, having heard of Juliet's

692 **forgot** i.e., neglected to mention 693 **to** compared to 694 **in thine
age** in all your life 696 **ruth** regret 697 **fere** mate 698 **before . . . a
year** a year earlier, I dare say 701 **iwis** certainly 702 **set light by** set
little value on 703 **could** would have

supposed death and having sought out poison from an
apothecary, returns from Mantua to Verona, he proceeds at
once with lantern and digging instruments to Juliet's
tomb.]

And then our Romeus, the vault stone set upright,
Descended down, and in his hand he bare the
    candlelight.   2630
And then with piteous eye the body of his wife
He gan behold, who surely was the organ of his life,
For whom unhappy now he is, but erst was blist.
He watered her with tears, and then an hundred
    times her kissed,
And in his folded arms full straitly he her plight,   2635
But no way could his greedy eyes be fillèd with her
    sight.
His fearful hands he laid upon her stomach cold,
And them on divers parts beside the woeful wight did
    hold.   2638
But when he could not find the signs of life he
    sought,
Out of his cursèd box he drew the poison that he
    bought.
Whereof he greedily devoured the greater part,
And then he cried with deadly sigh, fetched from his
    mourning heart:
"O Juliet, of whom the world unworthy was,
From which, for world's unworthiness, thy worthy
    ghost did pass,
What death more pleasant could my heart wish to
    abide
Than that which here it suffereth now, so near thy
    friendly side?
Or else so glorious tomb how could my youth have
    craved
As in one selfsame vault with thee haply to be
    engraved?
What epitaph more worth, or half so excellent,
To consecrate my memory could any man invent

2630 bare bore   **2635 straitly** tightly. **plight** folded, embraced
2638 wight person

As this our mutual and our piteous sacrifice
Of life, set light for love?" But while he talketh in
   this wise,
And thought as yet awhile his dolors to enforce,   2653
His tender heart began to faint, pressed with the
   venom's force,
Which little and little gan to overcome his heart.
  And whilst his busy eyne he threw about to every
   part,
He saw hard by the corpse of sleeping Juliet
Bold Tybalt's carcass dead, which was not all
   consumèd yet,
To whom, as having life, in this sort speaketh he: 2659
"Ah, cousin, dear Tybalt, whereso thy restless sprite
   now be,
With stretchèd hands to thee for mercy now I cry,
For that before thy kindly hour I forcèd thee to die.   2662
But if with quenchèd life not quenchèd be thine ire,
But with revenging lust as yet thy heart be set on
   fire,
What more amends or cruel wreak desirest thou   2665
To see on me than this which here is showed forth to
   thee now?
Who reft by force of arms from thee thy living breath, 2667
The same with his own hand, thou seest, doth poison
   himself to death.
And, for he causèd thee in tomb too soon to lie,
Too soon also, younger than thou, himself he layeth
   by."
  These said, when he gan feel the poison's force
   prevail,
And little and little mastered life for aye began to fail, 2672
Kneeling upon his knees, he said with voice full low,
"Lord Christ, that so to ransom me descendedst long
   ago
Out of thy Father's bosom, and in the Virgin's womb
Didst put on flesh, O, let my plaint out of this hollow
   tomb

2653 his dolors to enforce to emphasize his griefs   **2659 as having life**
as if he (Tybalt) were still alive   **2662 kindly hour** natural time
2665 wreak vengeance   **2667 Who** he who   **2672 mastered life** the life
he tamed or defeated.   **for aye** forever

Pierce through the air, and grant my suit may favor
    find!
Take pity on my sinful and my poor afflicted mind.
For well enough I know this body is but clay,
Naught but a mass of sin, too frail and subject to
    decay."
Then, pressed with extreme grief, he threw with so
    great force
His overpressèd parts upon his lady's wailèd corse   2682
That now his weakened heart, weakened with
    torments past,
Unable to abide this pang, the sharpest and the last,
Remainèd quite deprived of sense and kindly
    strength;   2685
And so the long-imprisoned soul hath freedom won at
    length.

[The Friar finds Juliet awakening and tries to persuade her
to take up a life of religious seclusion, but flees, leaving her
alone.]

When Juliet saw herself left in the vault alone
That freely she might work her will—for let or stay
    was none—   2766
Then once for all she took the cause of all her harms,
The body dead of Romeus, and clasped it in her
    arms.
Then she, with earnest kiss, sufficiently did prove
That more than by the fear of death she was attaint
    by love.   2770
And then, past deadly fear—for life ne had she care—   2771
With hasty hand she did draw out the dagger that he
    ware.   2772
"O, welcome, Death," quoth she, "end of
    unhappiness,
That also art beginning of assurèd happiness!

2682 **His overpressèd parts** his afflicted body. (He falls upon her body.)
wailèd bewailed   2685 **kindly** natural

2766 **let or stay** hindrance   2770 **attaint** infected, affected   2771 **ne had
she** she had no   2772 **ware** wore

Fear not to dart me now; thy stripe no longer stay.   ²⁷⁷⁵
Prolong no longer now my life; I hate this long delay.
For straight my parting sprite, out of this carcass
   fled,   ²⁷⁷⁷
At ease shall find my Romeus' sprite among so many
   dead.
And thou, my loving lord, Romeus, my trusty fere,   ²⁷⁷⁹
If knowledge yet do rest in thee, if thou these words
   dost hear,
Receive thou her whom thou didst love so lawfully,
That caused, alas, thy violent death, although
   unwillingly,
And therefore willingly offers to thee her ghost
To th' end that no wight else but thou might have just
   cause to boast
Th' enjoying of my love which aye I have reserved
Free from the rest, bound unto thee that hast it well
   deserved;
That so our parted sprites, from light that we see
   here,   ²⁷⁸⁷
In place of endless light and bliss may ever live
   yfere!"   ²⁷⁸⁸
This said, her ruthless hand through girt her valiant
   heart.   ²⁷⁸⁹
Ah, ladies, help with tears to wail the lady's deadly
   smart!

[The poem's final scene centers, as in Shakespeare's play,
on the Friar's narrative of events and the reconciliation of
the two grieving families.]

Text based on *The Tragical History of Romeus and Juliet, written First in Italian by Bandell and Now in English by Ar. Br. . . .* [1562].

2775 dart pierce with a dart. **stripe** blow. **stay** hold back
2777 straight straightway, at once **2779 fere** mate **2787 parted** departed. **from** departed from **2788 yfere** together **2789 ruthless** unsparing. **through girt** thrust through

In the following, departures from the original text appear in boldface; original readings are in roman.

30 Capilet Capelet   **192 beholding** behelding   **212 sport** port   **213 scarcely** skasely   **220 rapt** wrapt   **260 swaddling** swathing   **268 grafted** graffed   **282 not** no   **283 wrapped** rapt   **306 outward** vtwerd   **312 leisureless** lay sureles   **348 hands** hand   **666 chat** that   **2682 corse** corpse

Further Reading

Auden, W. H. "Introduction." *Romeo and Juliet*. The Laurel Shakespeare, gen. ed. Francis Fergusson, with a modern commentary by W. H. Auden. New York: Dell, 1958. Auden views *Romeo and Juliet* as a tragedy of "Fate, Choice, and Chance," though his discussion of the play emphasizes the culpability of both the lovers and the community of Verona. The feuding families create an atmosphere that encourages the lovers' self-absorption, and the lovers' decision to take their own lives is, for Auden, "in the profoundest sense, a failure of love, a proof of selfishness."

Brooke, Nicholas. *"Romeo and Juliet." Shakespeare's Early Tragedies*. London: Methuen, 1968. For Brooke, *Romeo and Juliet* is not an immature play but, in large part, a play about immaturity. The lovers' emotional attitudes, familiar from the Renaissance sonnet tradition, are qualified by the play's language and structure.

Calderwood, James L. *"Romeo and Juliet:* A Formal Dwelling." *Shakespearean Metadrama*. Minneapolis: Univ. of Minnesota Press, 1971. Calderwood explores through his metadramatic perspective an analogy between the lovers' search for an authentic language of feeling and Shakespeare's search for an authentic dramatic style. Ultimately, Calderwood argues, the lovers are unable to find a language that can do any more than leave them isolated in the purity and privacy of their love; Shakespeare, however, discovers in the formal organization of his play a means of reconciling the public and private dimensions of language.

Charlton, H. B. "Experiment and Interregnum." *Shakespearian Tragedy*. Cambridge: Cambridge Univ. Press, 1948. Charlton's influential essay argues that *Romeo and Juliet* was experimental both in its subject matter—its focus on fictional, unheroic young lovers rather than on public figures drawn from history—and in its emphasis upon fate as the driving force of the tragic action. Fate, working through the agency of the feud, movingly brings the lovers to their doom. Nonetheless, Charlton argues,

Shakespeare does not repeat this experiment with a tragedy of fate, seeking in his later tragedies less arbitrary
motives for the tragic action.

Coleridge, Samuel Taylor. *"Romeo and Juliet." Coleridge's
Writings on Shakespeare*, ed. Terence Hawkes. New York:
G. P. Putnam's Sons, 1959. Though an early play, *Romeo
and Juliet*, for Coleridge, gives evidence of both the or-
ganic structure and the strong sense of character found
fully developed in Shakespeare's mature art. Coleridge
admires the play's presentation of the passion of love, as
it develops from its origin in Romeo's sense of insufficiency, demanding the completion of a beloved, to his discovery of Juliet and a love that, though violent, is true and
pure.

Dickey, Franklin M. *Not Wisely but Too Well: Shakespeare's
Love Tragedies*, pp. 63–117. San Marino, Calif.: Hun-
tington Library, 1957. Examining *Romeo and Juliet*
against the background of its sources and Elizabethan literary and philosophical treatments of fate and love,
Dickey discovers moral patterns that qualify the attrac-
tiveness of the lovers. For Dickey, the play is a tragedy of
character, as the lovers, in their inability to control their
passionate love and grief, become subject to a fate that
operates as the agent of the moral order that they trans-
gress.

Evans, Bertrand. "Fate as Practicer: *Romeo and Juliet*."
Shakespeare's Tragic Practice. Oxford: Clarendon Press;
New York: Oxford Univ. Press, 1979. Evans is concerned
with the differences established between an audience's
understanding of the events of a play and the characters'
own perceptions. In *Romeo and Juliet*, these differences
are established from the beginning by the Chorus: we are
immediately given an awareness of the play's logic that is
denied to the characters, allowing us to see the play's in-
cidents not in isolation but as stages in the progress of
fate toward ending the feud.

Evans, Robert O. *The Osier Cage*. Lexington, Ky.: Univ. of
Kentucky Press, 1966. Evans's short book examines the
rhetorical style of *Romeo and Juliet*, focusing especially
upon the use of oxymoron that, as a figure yoking dis-
jointed elements, seems particularly suited to the play's
concerns. Evans considers how rhetorical patterns relate

to and reveal both character and action, suggesting that finally what is tragic in the play is neither character nor fate, but life itself, with its inevitable hostility to youth and to love.

Granville-Barker, Harley. *"Romeo and Juliet." Prefaces to Shakespeare*, 1946. Rpt. Princeton, N.J.: Princeton Univ. Press, 1963. Granville-Barker's sensitivity to the theatrical possibilities of *Romeo and Juliet* leads him to admire its strengths and also to note its immaturity. Unlike the mature tragedies, it is a play shaped by circumstance rather than by character, though he sees how, in the portrayal of the lovers, Shakespeare succeeds in making their fate seem inevitable rather than merely the result of ill luck.

Hazlitt, William. "Romeo and Juliet." *Characters of Shakespear's Plays*, 1817. London: Oxford Univ. Press, 1966. Hazlitt enthusiastically praises the play for its accurate portrayal of youthful passion. The love of Romeo and Juliet becomes, for Hazlitt, evidence of the truth and power of the imagination. The lovers are led to their exuberant delight not by what they have experienced of love but by what they hope for, and they die when they are unwilling to live without the vibrant hope that has made their lives valuable.

Kahn, Coppélia. "Coming of Age in Verona." In *The Woman's Part: Feminist Criticism of Shakespeare*, ed. Carolyn Ruth Swift Lenz, Gayle Greene, and Carol Thomas Neely. Urbana, Ill.: Univ. of Illinois Press, 1980. Kahn focuses on the feud as the primary tragic force within the play. Polarizing all social relations in Verona and demanding that masculinity find expression only in aggression, the feud insists that the lovers' union can be achieved only in death. The lovers' deaths, Kahn finds, are not fated but willed, acts of assertion over the destructive codes of patriarchal Verona that would keep them apart.

Lawlor, John. *"Romeo and Juliet."* In *Early Shakespeare*, ed. John Russell Brown and Bernard Harris, Stratford-upon-Avon Studies 3. London: Edward Arnold, 1961; New York: Schocken, 1966. Lawlor considers *Romeo and Juliet* in the tradition of medieval rather than classical tragedy to explore and explain the play's emphasis upon transcendent love. Like its medieval forebears, the play moves beyond the spectacle of suffering to an awareness of a happiness beyond time's reach. The play, Lawlor argues, thus both acknowledges and resists time's power, as the lovers in death at last find themselves together beyond the world of challenge and change.

Levin, Harry. "Form and Formality in *Romeo and Juliet*." *Shakespeare Quarterly* 11 (1960): 3–11. Rpt. in *Shakespeare and the Revolution of the Times*. New York: Oxford Univ. Press, 1976. Levin explores the tension between the immature and unrealistic emotional attitudes expressed by the play's elaborate formal patterning and the authentic dimension of feeling discovered by the lovers as they repudiate the artificial language and emotional codes they have inherited. In the tragedy, as Levin finds, the lovers are unable to sustain their private world: the patterns that the lovers seek to break through break them in the end.

Mahood, M. M. "*Romeo and Juliet.*" *Shakespeare's Wordplay*. London: Methuen, 1957. As the title of her book suggests, Mahood examines the wordplay of *Romeo and Juliet* as it articulates and organizes the play's tragic concerns. The ambiguities, tensions, and contradictions of the play's puns express the equilibrium achieved between the value of the lovers' experience and the awareness that it cannot be either permanent or perfect.

Nevo, Ruth. "*Romeo and Juliet.*" *Tragic Form in Shakespeare*. Princeton, N.J.: Princeton Univ. Press, 1972. In tracing the play's five-act structure, Nevo finds that *Romeo and Juliet* displays a continuous unfolding action, based on classical models of tragic form. With the reversal of their fortunes, the lovers move through the stages of tragic awareness to an acceptance of death as an assertion of their freedom and fidelity.

Peterson, Douglas L. "*Romeo and Juliet* and the Art of Moral Navigation." In *Pacific Coast Studies in Shakespeare*, ed. Thelma N. Greenfield and Waldo F. McNeir. Eugene, Oreg.: Univ. of Oregon Books, 1966. Arguing against a romantic view of the play, Peterson discovers the lovers' responsibility for their tragic fate in their repudiation of divine and rational guidance. Peterson examines the play's images of navigation and finds that they reveal the lovers' impatient commitment to a course guided only by blind passion and ending on the rocks of despair.

Rabkin, Norman. "Eros and Death." *Shakespeare and the Common Understanding.* New York: Free Press, 1967. Rabkin explores the play's paradoxical vision: the tragic action confirms the destructive irrationality of the lovers' passion, but at the same time the conventional logic of restraint and rationality seems impoverished next to the lovers' intensity. The play, Rabkin finds, articulates the tragic paradox of love itself: a yearning for completion and perfection that can be fully satisfied only by death.

Ribner, Irving. "Then I Denie You Starres: A Reading of *Romeo and Juliet.*" In *Studies in English Renaissance Drama: In Memory of Karl Julius Holzknecht,* ed. Josephine W. Bennett, Oscar Cargill, and Vernon Hall, Jr. New York: New York Univ. Press, 1959. Rpt. and rev. in *Patterns in Shakespearean Tragedy.* New York: Barnes and Noble, 1960. For Ribner, *Romeo and Juliet* affirms a Christian view of man's position in an ultimately benevolent and harmonious universe. The lovers are born into a world tainted by an evil for which they are not responsible and from which they are unable to escape. The play, Ribner argues, traces their growth toward an acceptance of death as a necessary means to the perfection they seek.

Snow, Edward. "Language and Sexual Difference in *Romeo and Juliet.*" In *Shakespeare's "Rough Magic": Renaissance Essays in Honor of C. L. Barber,* ed. Peter Erickson and Coppélia Kahn. Newark, Del.: Univ. of Delaware Press, 1985. Examining the lovers' language of emotion, Snow finds that it reveals the linking of their imaginations in "the same idiom," but it also reveals significant differences in their emotional responses. They inhabit, he finds, "separate worlds of desire": the universe generated by Romeo's desire is dominated by sight and is subject to greater rational control than is Juliet's world, which reflects a greater unity of feeling.

Snyder, Susan. "*Romeo and Juliet:* Comedy into Tragedy." *Essays in Criticism* 20 (1970): 391–402. Rpt. and rev. in *The Comic Matrix of Shakespeare's Tragedies.* Princeton, N.J.: Princeton Univ. Press, 1979. Snyder attends sensitively to the structure of the play and finds it unique among the tragedies in that it *becomes* rather than *is* tragic. Until Mercutio dies in Act 3, Snyder argues, the play is essentially comic, but with his death the play reverses its comic movement and the lovers find themselves in a new world of tragic responsibility.

Spurgeon, Caroline F. E. *Shakespeare's Imagery, and What It Tells Us*, pp. 310–316. Cambridge: Cambridge Univ. Press, 1935. Spurgeon traces the dominant imagery in *Romeo and Juliet* of light in its various forms: sun, moon, stars, lightning, fires, etc. The recurring images transform what might be obvious and conventional similes into a significant pattern of imagery that articulates the tragic action, as the brightness of Romeo and Juliet's love is suddenly extinguished.

Wells, Stanley. "Juliet's Nurse: The Uses of Inconsequentiality." In *Shakespeare's Styles*, ed. Philip Edwards, Inga-Stina Ewbank, and G. K. Hunter. Cambridge: Cambridge Univ. Press, 1980. Wells examines the play's rich stylistic diversity, especially the ways in which verbal style serves as a guide to character. The clearest example of this, Wells finds, is the Nurse's speech in Act 1, scene 3, where Shakespeare's skill at conveying her mental processes through rhythm and diction marks an important step in his artistic development.

Memorable Lines

A pair of star-crossed lovers . . .   (CHORUS   Prologue.6)

Here's much to do with hate, but more with love.
                               (ROMEO   1.1.175)

I will make thee think thy swan a crow.   (BENVOLIO   1.2.89)

. . . Queen Mab hath been with you.
She is the fairies' midwife, and she comes
In shape no bigger than an agate stone . . .
                             (MERCUTIO   1.4.53–55)

                 True, I talk of dreams,
Which are the children of an idle brain,
Begot of nothing but vain fantasy.   (MERCUTIO   1.4.96–98)

For you and I are past our dancing days.   (CAPULET   1.5.32)

O, she doth teach the torches to burn bright!
It seems she hangs upon the cheek of night
As a rich jewel in an Ethiop's ear—
Beauty too rich for use, for earth too dear!
                             (ROMEO   1.5.45–48)

You kiss by th' book.   (JULIET   1.5.111)

My only love sprung from my only hate!
Too early seen unknown, and known too late!
                        (JULIET   1.5.139–140)

He jests at scars that never felt a wound.   (ROMEO   2.2.1)

But soft, what light through yonder window breaks?
It is the east, and Juliet is the sun.   (ROMEO   2.2.2–3)

O Romeo, Romeo, wherefore art thou Romeo?
                          (JULIET   2.2.33)

What's in a name? That which we call a rose
By any other word would smell as sweet.

(JULIET   2.2.43–44)

Lady, by yonder blessèd moon I vow,
That tips with silver all these fruit-tree tops—

(ROMEO   2.2.107–108)

O, swear not by the moon, th' inconstant moon,
That monthly changes in her circled orb,
Lest that thy love prove likewise variable.

(JULIET   2.2.109–111)

Love goes toward love as schoolboys from their books,
But love from love, toward school with heavy looks.

(ROMEO   2.2.157–158)

How silver-sweet sound lovers' tongues by night,
Like softest music to attending ears!   (ROMEO   2.2.166–167)

Good night, good night! Parting is such sweet sorrow
That I shall say good night till it be morrow.

(JULIET   2.2.185–186)

Two such opposèd kings encamp them still
In man as well as herbs—grace and rude will;
And where the worser is predominant,
Full soon the canker death eats up that plant.

(FRIAR LAURENCE   2.3.27–30)

               Pronounce this sentence then:
Women may fall, when there's no strength in men.

(FRIAR LAURENCE   2.3.79–80)

These violent delights have violent ends
And in their triumph die, like fire and powder,
Which as they kiss consume.   (FRIAR LAURENCE   2.6.9–11)

Too swift arrives as tardy as too slow.

(FRIAR LAURENCE   2.6.15)

so light a foot
Will ne'er wear out the everlasting flint.
(FRIAR LAURENCE 2.6.16–17)

A plague o' both your houses!
They have made worm's meat of me.
(MERCUTIO 3.1.105–106)

Mercy but murders, pardoning those that kill.
(PRINCE 3.1.196)

Gallop apace, you fiery-footed steeds,
Towards Phoebus' lodging! (JULIET 3.2.1–2)

O serpent heart, hid with a flowering face! (JULIET 3.2.73)

Adversity's sweet milk, philosophy . . .
(FRIAR LAURENCE 3.3.55)

Hang up philosophy!
Unless philosophy can make a Juliet. (ROMEO 3.3.57–58)

It was the lark, the herald of the morn. (ROMEO 3.5.6)

JULIET
O, now begone! More light and light it grows.
ROMEO
More light and light, more dark and dark our woes!
(3.5.35–36)

Then window, let day in, and let life out. (JULIET 3.5.41)

Past hope, past cure, past help! (JULIET 4.1.45)

Not stepping o'er the bounds of modesty. (JULIET 4.2.27)

Then I defy you, stars! (ROMEO 5.1.24)

Beauty's ensign yet
Is crimson in thy lips and in thy cheeks,
And death's pale flag is not advanced there.
(ROMEO 5.3.94–96)

For never was a story of more woe
Than this of Juliet and her Romeo.   (PRINCE   5.3.309–310)

Contributors

DAVID BEVINGTON, Phyllis Fay Horton Professor of Humanities at the University of Chicago, is editor of *The Complete Works of Shakespeare* (Scott, Foresman, 1980) and of *Medieval Drama* (Houghton Mifflin, 1975). His latest critical study is *Action Is Eloquence: Shakespeare's Language of Gesture* (Harvard University Press, 1984).

DAVID SCOTT KASTAN, Professor of English and Comparative Literature at Columbia University, is the author of *Shakespeare and the Shapes of Time* (University Press of New England, 1982).

JAMES HAMMERSMITH, Associate Professor of English at Auburn University, has published essays on various facets of Renaissance drama, including literary criticism, textual criticism, and printing history.

ROBERT KEAN TURNER, Professor of English at the University of Wisconsin–Milwaukee, is a general editor of the New Variorum Shakespeare (Modern Language Association of America) and a contributing editor to *The Dramatic Works in the Beaumont and Fletcher Canon* (Cambridge University Press, 1966–).

JAMES SHAPIRO, who coedited the bibliographies with David Scott Kastan, is Assistant Professor of English at Columbia University.

♣

JOSEPH PAPP, one of the most important forces in theater today, is the founder and producer of the New York Shakespeare Festival, America's largest and most prolific theatrical institution. Since 1954 Mr. Papp has produced or directed all but one of Shakespeare's plays—in Central Park, in schools, off and on Broadway, and at the Festival's permanent home, The Public Theater. He has also produced such award-winning plays and musical works as *Hair, A Chorus Line, Plenty,* and *The Mystery of Edwin Drood,* among many others.